DISARMAMENT:
THE HUMAN FACTOR

Other Titles of Interest

BARNABY, F.
Prospects for Peace

CANNIZZO, C.
The Gun Merchants

CLOSE, R.
Europe Without Defense?

DOUGLASS J. D., Jr.
Soviet Military Strategy in Europe

FELD, B. T.
A Voice Crying in the Wilderness

FELD, W. J.
Western Europe's Global Reach

GROMYKO, A. A.
Only for Peace

HARKAVY, R. E.
Great Power Competition for Overseas Bases

JAPAN NATIONAL PREPARATORY COMMITTEE
A Call from Hibakusha of Hiroshima and Nagasaki

JOLLY, R.
Disarmament and World Development

LEBEDEV, N. I.
A New Stage in International Relations

LONG, F. A. and REPPY, J.
The Genesis of New Weapons

NOEL-BAKER, P.
The First World Disarmament Conference 1932–1933

TAYLOR, R. and PRITCHARD, C.
The Protest Makers

DISARMAMENT: THE HUMAN FACTOR

Proceedings of a Colloquium on the Societal Context for Disarmament, sponsored by UNITAR and Planetary Citizens and held at the United Nations, New York

Edited by

Ervin Laszlo and Donald Keys

PERGAMON PRESS

OXFORD • NEW YORK • TORONTO • SYDNEY • PARIS • FRANKFURT

U.K.	Pergamon Press Ltd., Headington Hill Hall, Oxford OX3 0BW, England
U.S.A.	Pergamon Press Inc., Maxwell House, Fairview Park, Elmsford, New York 10523, U.S.A.
CANADA	Pergamon Press Canada Ltd., Suite 104, 150 Consumers Rd., Willowdale, Ontario M2J 1P9, Canada
AUSTRALIA	Pergamon Press (Aust.) Pty. Ltd., P.O. Box 544, Potts Point, N.S.W. 2011, Australia
FRANCE	Pergamon Press SARL, 24 rue des Ecoles, 75240 Paris, Cedex 05, France
FEDERAL REPUBLIC OF GERMANY	Pergamon Press, GmbH, 6242 Kronberg-Taunus, Hammerweg 6, Federal Republic of Germany

First edition 1981

British Library Cataloguing in Publication Data

Colloquium on the Societal Context for
Disarmament, New York, 1978
Disarmament.
1. Disarmament - Congresses
I. Title   II. Laszlo, Ervin
III. Keys, Donald
327'.174   JX1974   80-41773

ISBN   0-08-024703-2   (Hardcover)
ISBN   0-08-028129-X   (Flexicover)

Printed in the United States of America

Preface

The chapters in this volume are based on papers that were first presented and discussed at a pathbreaking series of meetings at United Nations Headquarters between October 31 and December 1, 1978. The series constituted the symposium on disarmament, jointly organized by Planetary Citizens, a nongovernmental organization affiliated with the United Nations, and UNITAR, The United Nations Institute for Training and Research. The events attracted considerable attention in the United Nations. The Secretary-General sent his best wishes for successful deliberations, which were opened by Dr. Davidson Nicol, UN Under-Secretary-General and executive director of UNITAR. Several ambassadors took a prominent role in the proceedings, among them Ambassador Fereydoun Hoveyda of Iran, Ambassador Piero Vinci of Italy, and Carlos P. Romulo, Secretary of State for Foreign Affairs of the Philippines. The first of these events took place in the Dag Hammarskjöld Auditorium, and the next two in Conference Room 7, traditionally the hub of important international negotiations.

These externalities have more than a symbolic significance; indeed, they are part of the "message" of the chapters that follow. The heart of the UN system in New York is the scene of important but usually tedious negotiations, liberally interspersed with long-winded oratory, often with little novelty in content. In the formal sessions of the General Assembly, its six committees, and of other committees, commissions, and intergovernmental bodies, issues of the greatest importance are negotiated, or at least debated, but usually with the constraints from which contacts between sovereign states normally suffer. It is well said that our age is one of galloping change but creeping diplomacy.

The proceedings at the UNITAR–Planetary Citizens symposium provided a sharp and welcome contrast to all this. In the solemn UN conference room, the participants' nameplates had their names on them rather than that of a country or an organization. The participants spoke candidly, crisply, and to the point. The discussions were animated and infused with an excitement generated by the realization that, at last, the much neglected yet truly essential issues of disarmament and security were being addressed. Although the language was unofficial, it was not undiplomatic. There was a consensus that the problems of disarmament are universal and that all states bear responsibility both for the current impasse and for undertaking the initiatives needed for a breakthrough.

Many of those present came away feeling that if more of the spirit of free and dedicated deliberations exhibited at the symposium would infuse the official forums of negotiations on disarmament, objectives could be more sharply defined and progress toward them could be accelerated. If the spirit of this symposium would spread, not only the efficiency of the United Nations, but the chances of lasting peace and security in the world, would be enhanced.

It is practically impossible, and in any case not necessary, to summarize the rich variety of ideas and analyses presented and discussed at the meetings. The chapters that follow speak for themselves. But a few insights generated by the discussants could and should be conveyed. Perhaps foremost among these was the shared belief that disarmament is not primarily a military matter, nor solely a political one. While it is the generals and the statesmen who must implement it, the real prospects for achieving disarmament do not rest with them. The prospects must grow from roots deep in the thinking and values of all people, in all walks of life, in all societies.

In this connection, a major value shift is required. As long as the people of the world perceive a direct correlation between levels of armaments and national security, the process of disarmament will eliminate from national arsenals only those weapons which no military establishment really wants or needs. A qualitative escalation of "efficient" weapons and systems will continue in order to assure that "our" side is as least as strong as "theirs." Yet the resulting balance of terror does not assure lasting peace; merely the temporary absence of war. In an unregulated international environment, arms can no more assure peace than could guns in the saloons of the wild West. Where each can take the law into his own hands, the brandishing of arms is an invitation to a shoot-out. As long as contemporary powers behave as if they were in a frontier establishment where each is on his own, arm themselves with the best guns they can afford, and practice to draw quickly and shoot from the hip, they will be courting wars, small and large, local and global.

These are perceptions which are seldom spelled out and practically never discussed in the context of official negotiations on disarmament. Yet they may be crucial to assure the negotiations' success. Our values and perceptions in regard to territorial defense and national security have hardly changed in centuries. But the conditions under which security can be attained have altered radically, even in the past few years. Hence there is the need to bring up the issue of "human factors" in the debates on disarmament, which may well spell the difference between war and peace; even between survival and mass genocide.

The chapters that follow discuss and illuminate diverse aspects of the role of such human factors in the process of disarmament. Those that make up Part I provide a general review of the many human elements that underlie the current failure of the international community to make adequate progress toward the ultimate goal of general and complete disarmament. Part II considers more specifically the role of global community values as decisive factors in a broad-based support movement for disarmament, suggesting that a major value shift is essential if we are to create and maintain peace in an interdependent world. Part III analyzes some of the psychological and psychosocial elements that block effective movement toward disarmament and proposes strategies for coping with them. Part IV raises the basic question: If the arms race is not to be relied on for guaranteeing peace and security, what alternative mechanisms can we put in its place? Although political and institutional in regard to its objectives, this inquiry is likewise human-centered in substance, since the will to design a safe world depends in large part on the availability of reliable and attainable alternatives for assuring the security of states and maintaining world peace.

Parts II, III, and IV also include extracts from the lively discussions that followed the presentation of each set of papers at the symposium.

We wish to take this opportunity to thank all the participants in the symposium for their enthusiasm, their wisdom, and their generosity in having donated their time and energy to our common cause. We are grateful to the officers and supporting staff of our respective organizations, UNITAR and Planetary Citizens, for their support and contribution. And our sincere thanks go to all those who, in the UN secretariat as well as among member state missions, helped to make the series of events possible. We hope that through the publication of this volume the spread of the spirit of open and constructive humanism will be assisted inside as well as outside the United Nations.

Contents

ix

Contents

Part I

Introductory Survey:
The Neglected Human
Factors of Disarmament

1
Introduction

Davidson Nicol

On the last day of "United Nations Disarmament Week" in 1978 we held a joint panel discussion on neglected aspects of disarmament, arranged as an integral part of the joint symposium on disarmament planned by Planetary Citizens and UNITAR.

We were fortunate to have on our panel distinguished authorities in this field. Mrs. Inga Thorsson's second phase of involvement in the work of the United Nations brought her back to the international community not only as an Under-Secretary of State of Sweden responsible for disarmament and related matters, but as an international leader in this field whose voice is heard in nongovernmental circles as well. Having been in charge of Social Development and Humanitarian Affairs at the United Nations as well as in Sweden, Mrs. Thorsson is in a position to give us unique insights into "humanizing the approach to disarmament." The human element has been one of the main aspects neglected in the perennial debate on disarmament.

After the complex issues of disarmament have been subjected to rational analysis, and as progress is envisaged in negotiations toward a mutually secure and mutually advantageous path to disarmament, brakes are applied indicating the absence of a "political will" to move ahead. Professor Ervin Laszlo of UNITAR addressed himself to the detrimental effects of prevailing obsolete values and perceptions, an important aspect that is often neglected in the disarmament debate. He explains how the incongruity between existing values and beliefs about development, welfare, and security, on the one hand, and the new condition of global interdependence, on the other, have so far made it impossible for political leaders to commit themselves to real disarmament.

Donald Keys has been an active leader of a nongovernmental organization dedicated to the cause of international peace, development, and the promotion of human rights. As president of Planetary Citizens, he has not only long advocated the cause of disarmament in international forums, but has been equally involved in scholarly research on the different aspects of the disarmament debate. He focuses on those aspects of disarmament (besides weapons and other military hardware) which are often merely mentioned in passing during the disarmament debate. The "unexamined software" aspects are quite

3

vast, ranging from various proposed measures to build mutual confidence and political support for arms control, to measures of international regulation and peacekeeping in a disarming and disarmed world. Another aspect examined concerns the military "brain drain" and the "resource drain" suffered by the civilian sector of society, the reversal of which is extremely difficult because of entrenched vested interests and lack of adequate attention to the issue of conversion to peace.

If we look at the disarmament debates themselves, we see constant references to the problem of halting weapons testing, especially regarding nuclear warheads. But little is said about restraints in research and development in the military field. Yet the potential impact of ever-newer military technologies has been the nightmare of those who have dedicated their efforts to finding acceptable formulas for halting and reversing the arms race. William Epstein, formerly head of the United Nations Disarmament Branch and at present a UNITAR Special Fellow, writes on the impact of new technologies as a neglected aspect of disarmament. Mr. Epstein was a member of the Canadian delegation to the Special Session on Disarmament and a member of the delegation to the 33rd session of the Assembly, and his active voice on the non-proliferation issue and other aspects is heard widely through his books, articles, and newspaper columns.

For my part, let me briefly highlight one important aspect of disarmament which deserves some attention—the conventional arms race and arms transfer to smaller countries. There was some discussion of the issue in the early 1960s as part of the negotiations for general and complete disarmament, but the debate was unfortunately abandoned, and only some aspects of the matter were kept alive in the different but related context of decolonization. All the major conflicts of the past thirty years have been fought with conventional weapons, and all in the countries of the Third World. The weapons used in Korea, Indochina, the Middle East, Southern Africa, the Horn of Africa, and elsewhere were produced and transferred by the major powers, often because of short-sighted political advantage or simply for profit. Ironically, even as the debates and negotiations for disarmament were being conducted continuously during the past two decades, the total military expenditures in the world doubled to reach over $400 billion per year. Although a proportion of this is devoted to nuclear armaments, the rate of increase and the spread of conventional weapons is staggering. To complicate matters, some countries in major conflict areas have been assisted to develop their own weapons industries. Some of the Third World countries have used their financial capacity or industrial potential to buy both arms and the weapons technology itself from the unrestricted arms markets of the world with the great wealth acquired through the sale of oil, gold, or uranium. This sometimes leads to the temptation of military adventurism—against neighboring countries or, in some cases, against very distant countries—because of political or religious zeal.

To illustrate the arms traffic, Tom Gervasi, in his book *Arsenal of Democracy* (New York: Grove Press, 1977), gives figures of arms supplied by the United States in five years between 1971 and 1975 to developing countries. They include 3,560 tanks and self-propelled guns, 5,240 armored cars, 63 fighting ships, 22 submarines, 593 supersonic combat aircraft, 460 helicopters, and more than 10,000 missiles of various types. The USSR is alleged in the first half of 1978 to have delivered to some African countries alone about 120,000 tons of military equipment, including vehicles, naval craft, planes and helicopters, and small arms and ammunition. The United States announced recently that it concluded arms sales in the amount of $13 billion. These figures of arms supplies from the United States and the USSR to developing countries may not be exact, but they give an estimate of the volume involved. All these arms evidently were not acquired for ceremonial parades or for agricultural development. The skill and amount of money involved in producing, buying, and using them could have brought about spectacular improvements in many of the poorer countries. Currently, half of the debts of developing countries are generated by arms purchases.

My emphasis here on the conventional arms race is meant to highlight a relatively neglected area. But this is not to say that we should not give priority to nuclear disarmament. A great danger in this regard is the proliferation of nuclear weapons, without the limiting factor of fear brought about by an accurate knowledge of the devastating consequences of their use. It must be admitted that, in some cases, the terror of political loneliness and the possibilities of destruction by neighbors have forced nations to regard the acquisition of nuclear weapons as their only hope for survival. It is the duty of the international community to provide safeguards for such nations by political treaty or some other means, which might include perhaps a sufficiency, but not a superfluity, of conventional weaponry. The citizens of any country need to feel that they will not be wiped off the face of the earth or be made permanent exiles.

Controlling factors that could be used by the governments of developed arms-manufacturing countries could include a refusal to share the transfer of technology of armaments and a selective control of the supply of spare parts. This can only be done internationally by agreement that those who contravene agreements can be isolated and, if need be, ostracized.

It is our belief at UNITAR that there is a real need for informal but informed discussion of the key issues of disarmament, for many of the aspects are as yet unexamined or are just coming to be examined. This book will examine the underlying root causes, rather than the resulting surface effects, of the arms problem. Ervin Laszlo of UNITAR and Donald Keys of Planetary Citizens first brought together the individual authors as a panel of experts that is unusual if not unprecedented in the breadth of its interdisciplinary scope and the depth of its knowledge. Such a panel is much needed today, since just as no nation can solve the major world problems of itself, the vexing problem of the arms race cannot be expected to yield to the wisdom of only one or another field of knowledge. We must surely marshal the tools and the capacities of all available fields in an integrated way if we are to achieve the goal of lifting the burden and the anxiety of the arms race from humanity.

The topics which will be discussed and the problems which will be examined are not ordinarily dealt with. Yet, I am convinced that they may be central to the dilemma of disarmament and that their inclusion as areas of major importance in planning and negotiating for disarmament is long overdue.

UNITAR has already demonstrated its active interest in this field by setting up an Institute of Disarmament in Geneva. One of its initial tasks will be to address itself to some of the issues raised in this symposium.

The real hope for addressing any of the complex issues underlying the problem of disarmament must lie in human beings themselves. It is they, and especially the young generation, who must learn to live peacefully in an interdependent world society. It is they who must evolve the values and adopt the perspectives suited to the new conditions under which we all live today and will continue to live in the coming decades. The organizers of the symposium and editors of this book are very conscious of this "human factor" and seek to draw attention to ways and means whereby its positive potentials could be mobilized for the cause of peace. It is my hope, shared by Ervin Laszlo and Donald Keys, that the symposium and this book may contribute to the clarification of the deep underlying roots of insecurity in the world, and that these issues may then increasingly find their way to discussions and negotiations in the established and now significantly enlarged forums on disarmament in the United Nations.

2

Humanizing the Approach to Disarmament

Inga Thorsson

The arms race now runs at a pace at which expenditures approach half a trillion dollars a year. The best brains that the evolution of man has produced are tenaciously occupied with the refinement of new means of destruction. The madness of this race to oblivion, as it may well prove to be, seems to elude comprehension. Since belief in the devil, to which the wickedness of the world could formerly be attributed, is outmoded, we shall have to look to ourselves for the causes of the present situation.

One could, of course, take a detached view of the problem and, with reference to biologists who tell us that there is nothing unique about mistakes in the never-ending evolutionary process on this earth, accept the notion that man may in the end prove himself to be an evolutionary mistake. Relative to each single species living today, ten to one hundred have perished. On the other hand, it is somehow comforting that man has one asset that is unique in comparison with his fellow species. This is the capacity for reasoning and learning; in short, his critical mind.

How is it that this critical mind seems to be idle when faced with the challenge to its very existence, represented by the stockpiles of new destructive weapons? In actual fact, it can be argued that today, with the exception of competent and dedicated but fairly small groups of people, worldwide public awareness in the field of armaments has fallen to an all-time low, in spite of unprecedented challenges. It may be remembered that the first international peace movement started off with broad public support in the 1870s after the French-German war. The 1950s saw fierce campaigns against the development of nuclear weapons.

In this perspective, it is difficult to avoid some questions: why is there no mass-movement today for nuclear disarmament? How can it be explained that there is no concern in the minds of people against the *neutron bomb*, perhaps the most perverted result so far of the restless efforts in armaments research and development? How can we explain the absence of mass protest against the

7

forty million fresh dollars poured into the military systems of the world every hour of every day?

I will suggest some factors at play which, if taken into account by those who are in a position to influence public opinion and reach out to people, could help to bring about a more promising outlook for disarmament. My first point has to do with perceptions. The definition of national security, as traditionally perceived and communicated to people, is less than adequate in today's world. True, from the point of view of national security, any armament step might appear to be rational. But in summing up the totality of all such seemingly rational decisions, we are provided with a picture of monumental irrationality.

National security is the primary objective of national politics; indeed, a cornerstone of the national state. Formerly, the objective of national security was met by military means. Since the Second World War, resource allocations to armaments have seen few restrictions, and they have been justified by referring to needs of the security of the nation and its people. But since the 1970s it has been increasingly obvious that national security can no longer be equated with military might.

The ultimate purpose of national security is to secure the independence and sovereignty of the national state, for assuring the freedom of its individual citizens—freedom to develop economically, socially, and culturally. Armed struggle has been, and in a few cases may still be, necessary to *acquire* this freedom. To *preserve* it, arms are not enough. The carefully guarded borders of a nation-state are no longer a guarantee for the security of its people, in the broader sense just defined.

Rather than a guarantee for national security, the arms race is one of the most imminent threats to the survival of humanity. Let me refer to these grave threats in terms of crude headlines:

- The arms race itself
- The present crisis of the main production systems of the world, including worldwide unemployment, worldwide inflation, the worldwide monetary crisis
- The energy crisis
- Threats to the environment and to the ecological balance
- Last, but not least, the threats emanating from the preservation of glaring economic and social inequalities between—and within—nations and the accompanying rise of North-South tensions.

These are threats against the security of nations and peoples and, overwhelmingly, are sources of want, poverty, and sufferings of individual human beings all over the world.

A second factor is the concept of a neutral, value-free science, which has led to the separation of reason and emotion, so characteristic of our societies today. Military research and development has, unfortunately, a prominent place today in science. And it seems as if military technology, moving forward at an accelerated speed, is pushed ahead by an invisible, dehumanized hand. It is gratifying in this respect that concerned citizens in many countries have engaged in a kind of technology assessment, in voicing fears that a continuous expansion of nuclear energy can lead to unbearable risks in the storage of nuclear wastes and in the accumulation of increasing amounts of plutonium. One would have wished, though, that the further proliferation of nuclear weapons had been a more important aspect of that debate.

A third factor also concerns difficulties of perception. More than thirty years of peace in Europe, although a very short period in European civilization, may lead to an erroneous feeling of safety. Erroneous it is, because the dynamism in arms development is a constant challenge to the stability of the balance of terror, which is not fail-safe in the first place; erroneous also because of the many wars that have raged on other continents.

Another point is that the armaments debate deals with facts and figures that, understandably, transcend what can easily be grasped by nonprofessionals in the field. Who can catch the proportions of a reality where the present worldwide storage of nuclear weapons corresponds to 1,300,000 Hiroshima bombs? And let us further agree that language itself has a tremendous power. Without it we would not have poetry, and probably not have wars. But language has been corrupted by means of the frequent euphemisms that have entered the vocabulary of the armaments community, such as "bonus kills" and "megadeath." This has the effect of throwing dust into peoples' eyes. Everybody knows what a cannon or a gun is. But what is the general cognitive value, one may ask, of a mini-nuke or a MIRV?

Part of this development is due to the very approach to disarmament adopted for practical purposes in the absence of general and complete disarmament: the step-by-step approach. With that approach, disarmament negotiations necessarily engage in highly technical matters and issues, which unfortunately tend to obscure the very purpose of the whole process. But we must always keep in mind that disarmament is too important to be left solely to experts and governments. We must be able to communicate with people in human terms, in order to get their indispensable support and demand for results.

Additionally, a situation in which masses of people see nothing but good entertainment in a film like *Dr. Strangelove* is not likely to lead to disarmament. On the other hand, there is also the possibility that the lack of palpable progress, a real breakthrough in the field, imposes a sense of despair on those who actually perceive the true nature of our present predicament.

Admittedly, in the present situation we are short of a credible model for a peaceful world. Some psychologists maintain that a non-armed peace would be experienced as a defenseless situation, and would therefore be dangerous because member nations of the international community do not yet know of any substitute for war as the last recourse in international relations. The necessary substitution for violence as the ultimate sanction in international conflicts seems to me to presuppose that national sovereignty be no longer associated with unlimited freedom in foreign policy. The first such freedom to be disposed of is the freedom to possess nuclear weapons.

The people constitute a tremendous potential force for peace and global security through disarmament. We must not stand in the way of this force by dehumanizing disarmament talks and negotiations. Parallel to all the technical debates, we must learn to talk clear and unequivocal language, and listen to clear and unequivocal language. Through humanizing the approach to disarmament, we might assist in overcoming the attitude of "I don't know and I don't care," which characterizes all too many people's thinking today. Since their own survival is at stake, they must be among those who now mobilize for disarmament and peace.

3

New Conditions and Obsolete Perceptions

Ervin Laszlo

It is a remarkable fact that there is hardly a government today that would not profess to favor disarmament. Yet, the world keeps arming itself at a madly accelerating rate. There is hardly any expert who would contest that we already have more weapons than are needed for any conceivable peacekeeping function and that a strategic balance at lower levels of armament is possible and desirable. Yet, spending on arms and the military continues to increase. It appears that we all want one thing, but do something else. Yet this is not Alice in Wonderland, but presumably the real world. Perhaps we failed to pay attention to the underlying reasons for the arms race. The vital but neglected aspects of disarmament include the whole issue of values and perceptions.

Is it possible that contemporary humanity at large, and especially the majority of national governments, suffer from what anthropologists call a "culture lag"? This is a lag in values, beliefs, perceptions, and conceptions compared with the evolution of objective societal conditions. It occurs whenever the tempo of change is faster in the economic, social, or political domain than in the culture, or when lack of information and education, or strong vested interests, prevent some classes or groups of people from perceiving changed conditions. This was the case in every major societal transformation in history from the neolithic to the industrial revolution. And it is occurring today in the process of industrialization of developing countries and in the process of "post-industrialization" of some developed ones. The masses, who have too little information on the new conditions, and the dominant elites, whose interests are vested in the previous order, fail to grasp the new context, and they fight the tides of change with increasingly obsolete values and behaviors. Such a culture lag affects all aspects of contemporary society on both national and international levels. It affects especially the process of disarmament, by preserving outmoded conceptions and policies of national and world security.

The culture lag always involves two poles: an objective pole constituted by economic and social conditions that exist regardless of whether or not they are

11

perceived, and a subjective pole, represented by the values and perceptions of people. Today, the objective conditions of society include the following factors:

- Interdependence of states, economies, social processes, and cultures
- Overdevelopment of military establishments compared with other sectors of society and overspending on arms and military research and development compared with spending on humanly beneficial sectors such as health, social services, and infrastructure
- Overexploitation of some nonrenewable natural resources, such as fossil fuels and industrially important metals and minerals
- Progressive impoverishment and despoilation of the environment, including loss of productive top soils, reduction of rain forests, desertification, and the various forms of urban and industrial pollution
- Overpopulation in certain rural regions, compared with the availability of local food potentials, and overpopulation of certain urban regions with respect to the availability of housing, employment, and basic social services
- Major and still growing income and production gaps between countries as well as within countries, making for the emergence of "dual economies" in and between countries
- The progressive disappearance of established cultures and means of self-identification of peoples in the face of the "coca-colonization" of the world by high-powered advertising and profit-motivated private interests
- Instabilities in the international economic and financial system, leading to the progressive loss of foreign exchange of the poorer countries, to worldwide inflation and unemployment, and to unused industrial capacities in some developed countries
- Major disparities in the scientific-technical potential of countries, and its further aggravation through the phenomenon of the "brain drain"

If we went into further detail, the list could be extended almost ad infinitum. But these key concepts suffice to highlight the new conditions of contemporary humanity. Hardly any of them were present as major factors in world affairs two decades ago, and some have emerged into prominence only in the last few years.

Contrasting with these new conditions, there are a number of still influential values and perceptions that have become obsolete. These include the following:

- The "survival-of-the-fittest" theory: Each man is for himself, and the strongest and most resourceful prosper while the weak go down.
- The "self-regulation" concept of the economy: There is an invisible hand that harmonizes individual and public interest so that everyone can look out for himself in the happy knowledge that this will automatically benefit others in his society.

- The "trickle-down" theory: Wealth inevitably penetrates from the richer to the poorer strata of society; so the best way to help the poor is for the rich to get still richer.
- The "efficiency cult": Maximum productivity for each person, each machine, and each organization is the ultimate goal and achievement.
- The "technological imperative": if something *can* be produced, it *must* be produced even if demand has to be created for it.
- The "economic man" image: People are purely economic actors, producers and consumers of goods and services, and their behavior can be computed in terms of these activities.
- "Consumerism": Social fulfilment is epitomized by having the greatest variety of consumer goods at the disposal of a mass public with adequate buying power.
- The "profit motive" concept of human nature: What people want is profit and wealth; everything else is but superficial window dressing.
- The "man, Lord of nature" image: Humanity has proved itself smarter than all the rest of nature and has an indisputable right to bend nature to his own will and benefit.

These values and perceptions are mostly economic and social in nature. They are closely allied, however, with political perceptions such as the following:

- The "survival-of-the-fittest" theory of the state (social Darwinism): Each State is for itself, and the strongest state triumphs by conquering and annexing the territories, peoples, and resources it needs for its survival.
- The "self-regulation" concept of international relations: There is a balance of power toward which international power configurations tend; this means that each state must attempt to maximize its own power, since its opponents will do the same, thus keeping the balance.
- The "trickle-down" theory of international wealth and development: The best chances of emerging from poverty for the less-developed countries lie in a strong and wealthy group of developed countries, who will spread wealth and the benefits of development to the rest.
- Westernism: All people, inasmuch as they manage to overcome their spiritual backwardness, want the things that modern Westerners want regardless of what customs their forefathers observed and where they go to pray on their holy days.
- Chauvinism—"My country, right or wrong": People are not to reason and question the actions of their country, but give it their undivided loyalty, even to the extent of dying for it if necessary.
- The "sovereign state" concept: All countries are sovereign and independent nation-states, accountable only to their own people and no one else.
- The "lifeboat ethic": Should there be another war or a major catastrophe,

we, at least, have the duty to survive and not be dragged down by others, for we must hand down the great accomplishments of humanity to future generations.

The thrust of the above values and perceptions is this: All people and all societies want wealth and power; all are out for themselves, and those that manage to get a good piece of the pie are the winners; ergo, our primary duty is to ourselves. On the happy assumption of an invisible hand, of the trickle-down effect, of the balance-of-power doctrine, and of the lifeboat ethic, fulfilling our duty to ourselves also benefits others. At least, there is no need to feel very guilty about being selfish.

In the expanding and relatively pristine world environment of the recent past, high degrees of egoism and chauvinism and much abuse of natural resources could be tolerated. Each could act to maximize its own interest; the negative consequences were relatively well absorbed while the positive spin-offs produced a self-righteous glow of being beneficial to the weak, the poor, and the backward. Conflicts arising from perceived or real injustices could be contained, and even the loser could usually recover, or move on. Such times are now definitely over. Local confrontations can flare into regional confla-grations and eventually into a global cataclysm. Measures that ensure short-term economic benefits—such as protectionism, price-maximizing cartels, competitiveness on all fronts, tied-aid measures, and political power-backed deals—aggravate existing disparities and feed tensions, threatening a break-down of the existing system of economic relationships. Mindless exploitation of nature and natural resources leads to nonviable environments and prema-ture shortages. Concentrations of wealth and power trigger countervailing movements to which even the wealthiest and most powerful are not immune.

But, as long as the kinds of perceptions enumerated here remain influential, nations will not disarm. The arms race will not slacken. Military research and development will continue. Funds will not be released from armaments and transferred to development. Protectionism, price wars, and all forms of eco-nomic pressures and unfair practices will persist. The poor will get poorer. The rich will get richer, although not for long. Injustice and inequity will domi-nate. And tensions will escalate so that it will be only a matter of time before the arsenals of mass destruction are put to their awful use.

Disarmament cannot occur in an insecure world; it is hopeless to pursue serious efforts toward it as long as the perceptions which lead to world insecurity are neglected. Disarmament is not purely or even primarily a military matter. First and foremost, it is a matter of perceptions and goals. It is as useless to ask a contemporary government to disarm itself as it was to ask a frontiersman in the California gold rush to do so. Governments perceive themselves as acting in a highly predatory international environment, regulat-ed only marginally if at all by law and justice. And as long as they thus perceive themselves, their perceptions will be justified.

How are we to break the vicious cycle of self-fulfilling prophecies? It is very likely that a major breakthrough would require the more or less simultaneous emergence of new perceptions in the majority of the world's governments. At the present time, their culture lag is due partly to the disproportionate influence of the military-technical establishment compared with independent scientists and intellectuals, and partly to the still low level of education and information of the general public. The powerful military and business elites reinforce obsolete perceptions, and the general population fails to counteract their influence. It is not surprising that the majority of governments operate on obsolete assumptions in their assessment of the basic issues of national and world security.

Perhaps governments would do well to listen to those well-informed groups in their·societies that have no vested interest in the status quo. If they did so, they would soon come to see what independent scientists and other intellectuals the world over are seeing with frightening force and clarity: that to maintain arms and delivery systems that can wipe the adversary off the face of the earth and to spend over $400 billion a year in further adding to and perfecting these capabilities is not only totally unnecessary, but sheer madness.

If the culture lag could be eliminated, or just reduced in a significant way, the problems of disarmament, which now appear so formidable, would become tractable. Expert studies show that almost all aspects of disarmament have politically, economically, and socially sound solutions, and the host of studies currently under way will no doubt add further to this storehouse of relevant information. The intractability of the problems lies not in their intrinsic nature, but in the perceptions of the decision makers. What is lacking is the political will. And it is precisely this element that could be added to negotiations on disarmament if the obsolete perceptions still dominating national thinking on the issues would give way to a more objective and informed assessment of the contemporary world situation. At least the following basic perceptions would need to gain influence:

- The "symbiosis" theory of human relationships: Humanity is not exempt from nature's rule that he who survives is not the most aggressive, but the most symbiotic and adaptive with respect to others and the environment.
- The "altruism is pragmatic" insight: In an interdependent situation, all long-term destinies coincide; one humanity, one destiny; we either hang together or we hang separately.
- The "unity in diversity" thesis: People and societies are and can be different culturally, economically, and politically, yet can respect one another and strive to maintain harmonious and mutually beneficial relations among themselves.
- The "multi-level loyalty" concept: It is not any less moral and possible for individuals and groups to profess loyalty to the world community as a

whole than it is to profess loyalty to their family, business, institution, community, culture, or religion. National and supranational loyalties do not conflict, but reinforce one another.

If insights such as these would become more widespread in the contemporary world, real progress could be made in the efforts to create a new international economic order, to meet basic human needs, and to eliminate economic and political injustices. And, at the same time, disarmament would become a real possibility. The updating of the international community's conceptual software is a necessary condition of reducing its military hardware. We should no longer neglect this fact.

4

The Neglected "Software" Aspects of Disarmament

Donald Keys

The greatest lack in the field of disarmament has been lack of progress in disarming. This deficit has by now become so obvious that it is time to question seriously the manner in which the problem is being approached. If there is any need to catalogue the failure to take actual steps in the direction of disarmament, perhaps the example of the test ban will serve well. After the exhaustive negotiations of the early sixties, the achieved ban exempted weapons tests underground and resulted in no essential diminution of the weapons race. After twenty years, a comprehensive ban still eludes us, and current possibilities suggest that we will be faced with a ban with major exemptions and time limits.

I wish to suggest that the current approach to disarmament is *symptomatic*. It deals with the nature and content of the arms race itself and focuses on types and capabilities of armaments, and to a certain extent on the problems of verification and inspection of any arms-limitation agreements. Only in the area of economic interaction with the arms race can it be said that we have looked at some of the more *causal* aspects of the question. We have become familiar with the momentum lent to the arms competition by the invested energies of the scientific and engineering communities, the armament industry, and the interrelated political and military sectors. We have also discovered that the redirection of energy away from the now famous vicious circle of the military-industrial-scientific-political complex is exceedingly difficult.

With this exception, and it is a major one, our interest in the arms race has remained essentially symptomatic, which may be a major reason for the frustration and disappointment that has accompanied our efforts of the fifties, sixties, and seventies. If we have been overemphasizing the hardware and symptomatic aspects of the arms race to the neglect of the "software" and causal aspects, what would the latter include? Together, the software aspects of disarmament would constitute the societal context in which the arms race is

17

proceeding. Massed human actions such as an arms race proceed out of the total mix of factors operative in the persistent societal context.

Although we may feel overwhelmed by the untidy task this perspective presents, we may come to feel that we have no alternative but to deal with the range of operative societal factors if we wish a definitive answer to the question, Why have we not achieved disarmament? Such factors would certainly include, but not be limited to, psychological perspectives, social attitudes, cultural uniqueness, philosophic and ideological notions, notions of national sovereignty versus world-system views, the question of a common world value system or its lack, and the question of achieving alternative methods of providing for peace and security in the absence of national arms and armies, which are now obviously becoming dysfunctional and counterproductive in the quest for security.

A causal or "software" approach to disarmament also flies in the face of present heavy commitment—the commitment of a large portion of the academic community to three decades of essentially bipolar examination of strategies, games, and hardware equivalencies. These examinations have surely made us more clever, but questions are beginning to be raised regarding the extent to which we have at the same time become more wise. Our gaming has tended to take place within the context of an assumption of an unending arms race of greater or lesser proportions—an assumption and a choice which leads to one set of strategies which may be quite at variance with those strategies which would be selected if the goals were major arms limitations or disarmament.

I should like to limit my present examination of "software" factors primarily to psychological attitudes and to the question of maintenance of international peace and security.

One of the psychological factors with which we have become somewhat familiar through its very obvious contributions to acceleration of arms competition is the concept of *threat perception*. How the supposed adversary is perceived is in fact very much more important than what his actual condition may be. Trust and confidence are shaken and insecurity is advanced by an increase in perceived threat. We are well aware of the "worst-possible-case" definitions regularly and dutifully supplied by military planners on every side to their policymakers and political leaders. Unfortunately, preparing for the worst, particularly if it is an unwarrantedly pessimistic reading of the motivations and goals of the supposed adversary, leads directly to the kind of provocative responses to real or unreal signals that precipitate, in any case, the perceived condition. The arms race owes substantial momentum to this "self-fulfilling prophecy." Borrowing a term from biology, this response might be called "mimicry." One side mimics the other because of worst-possible-case definitions. The MIRV'd missiles of one side are seen as laying the basis for a preemptive attack; at the same time, the development of civil defense measures and missiles with greater throw weight by the other side are seen as serving precisely the same end, while each party sees its own actions as eminently and obviously defensive in nature. Thus, development of cruise missiles by one side goes hand in hand with unexpectedly high production rates on the other. Responses made in kind justify and reinforce the original "worst-case" definitions.

A second major and related factor acting at psychological levels concerns *biased information reception*. Like individuals, nations as human collectives tend to accept information which reinforces what they already believe. Like us, they tend to reject or filter out information which would require a change in attitude and a changed understanding of the situation, particularly if it would imply major shifts or readjustments in the national life. Even if some state opts for actions which an outside observer would equate with a serious interest in disarmament, those very same steps are not likely to be read in that light by other members of the arms race, because the new information is being discounted or filtered out.

The *image* problem is also a major factor in the arms race, particularly in negotiations. States are preoccupied with a belief that they must adopt a stance that is seen as strong and forceful, in order not to tempt others to take advantage of them. The very same stance is, however, easily read by the other parties as being unyielding, intransigent, and indicative of an unwillingness to negotiate in good faith.

Dehumanization has always been an important factor in military contests and arms races. Historically, "the enemy" has been deprived of the characteristics of being human. The "out-group" has been denied the full range of feelings, loves, wants, and desires, and assigned the role of demons and butchers. In a similar manner, we tend to *project* onto the "out-group" characteristics of our own that are inconsistent with the image we wish to hold of ourselves. We tend also to *stereotype* the adversary in various ways—for instance, as being capable of much greater consistency than we and of being wholly rational and purposeful in sinister ways.

If psychological factors are indeed major conditioning contributors to adversary relationships and to the arms race, then it follows that strategies for arms limitation and disarmament must include agreements, steps, or initiatives that make good psychological sense and do not serve to exacerbate an existing situation.

Confidence-building measures or steps which portray one side to the other as the first side really wishes to be seen (as peaceloving, dependable, and consistent, but firm) will finally reap the reward of a change in perception or attitude on the part of the adversary. But to achieve the goal of "modified perception" on the part of others, the "signals" must be unambiguous over a period of time.

No major participant in the present nuclear arms race has yet opted to adopt a long-term strategy that is psychologically sound. There are, of course, any number of steps that any such party could take which would serve radically to alter the context in which the present contest is taking place, and many such steps are frequently mentioned as candidates for individual or joint action. One which has been revived lately by Canada is the suggestion for a cutoff of the production of fissionable materials for weapons purposes. Another is an individual moratorium on all nuclear weapons testing until achievement of a comprehensive test ban. Still another would be an announced end to production of nerve gases and their destruction in order to encourage and accelerate progress toward a chemical-weapon-ban treaty. No such steps would be any major threat to the security of the state executing them, but they would lend credibility to that state's position and would develop pressure for a response in kind.

There are a few recent examples of the effectiveness of nationally initiated measures of this kind. One such example concerns the achievement of a ban and adoption of a treaty on prohibition of biological and bacteriological weapons. In that instance, one government, that of the United States, announced that it was ending the production of such weapons and proceeding to destroy them. In the changed atmosphere, a treaty followed quickly. Another instance concerns the Cuban missile crisis. There were ambiguous signals in the air about the likely behavior and intentions of governments. One government specifically chose to select and act on the most friendly and least inimical feeler. The result was that an agreement became possible, and a major crisis was defused.

It is possible to suggest, therefore, that bringing psychological factors in the arms race to a new level of cognizance and awareness could result in the initiation of steps and measures that would have the effect of cooling off the contest, of reversing it, and of making progress in arms limitation and disarmament much more likely and possible.

In the particular instances described, it is not difficult to discern the relative security loss and gain factors. There might have been some small short-term reduction in security from a military point of view in the loss of the germ-warfare option. At the same time, the net gain in national and world security was of a high order, and could have been utilized to lead directly to further important and cognizable steps in disarmament.

Specific philosophic, ideological, and religious notions about the nature of the world and of man can also predetermine responses to changing situations, and in particular to the matter of security and arms. If a state holds that its view of the world and its future is the only correct one, and that it must protect those seeds of the future against all odds, it will adopt a different stance from states which together feel that the future design is unknown and must be sought. Thus, strong ideological or philosophic "sets" can predispose against common approaches to disarmament and provision of world security, and can in fact militate against common security. In order to overcome the suspicions of states that feel themselves entrusted with a uniquely valid approach to the future (and many do), they must be made secure in the notion that the uniqueness and common thread of their contribution will not be ignored (although its excesses and distortions will be).

Can world security (and therefore disarmament) be achieved without a minimal agreed global value system? If there is no common view of the nature of the human being and of what he should give to the community and receive from life, is there a base upon which a viable world society and security can be constructed? At every organized level of human society there is common assent to the basis of the society, which gives rise in turn to legal forms and finally to the institutions of the society. We may well ask whether a world society can evade these apparent requirements. If it cannot, then the societal base for security in the world community may be considerably weakened in the future.

The situation is not hopeless, however. The member states of the world community have agreed on many aspects of a global value system, particularly as embodied in the various instruments of human rights, in documents on a new international economic order, and in the funding of food, medical, housing, educational, and technical assistance programs on a world scale. These steps are either tacit or overt assent to an emerging global value system. That system, however, is as yet so weak through nonimplementation and scanty funding as to raise serious questions as to whether the world value base will support such serious and community-wide endeavors as general and complete disarmament.

Differences in social attitudes within nations and in national goals may also militate for or against disarmament. How nations regard restraint of individual and group aggression under legally defined parameters, and how they feel about violence and nonviolence between individuals and between nations, bears on their reaction to and reliable participation in arms agreements. How members of a society feel about what constitutes a justifiable means of achieving personal and national ends differs among countries and cultures.

I turn now to the question of security. There is in the international community, in the United Nations, and therefore also within nations, only the dimmest beginning of the notion that disarmament will have to be accompanied by a parallel development of alternative means for maintaining international peace and security. When arms and armies are no longer present, do we really believe that peace will be automatic and unbroken? The failure to erect alternative and effective means for peacekeeping and peaceful settlement of disputes has as a direct corollary the failure to achieve disarmament, or even major arms reductions.

The human condition is such that we routinely and systematically place active restraints on aggressive violence by human beings within every level of our societies, but we have yet to do so at the level of the world community. States, however, are not going to disarm in a circumstance in which they feel they have no alternative way to protect their vital interests and no way to provide defense and restraint of violence in a relatively anarchic and dangerous world. Various degrees of arms limitation may be achieved under present circumstances, which could result in helpful and welcome budget reductions. But substantial steps will not be taken unless states feel secure that their vital interests will be protected through other means if not by arms and armies in which, historically, they have always placed their faith. It can be stated without reasonable fear of contradiction that the present state of developments in the fields of peacekeeping and peacemaking at the international level and through the United Nations is precisely the measure of the degree of disarmament we can presently expect to achieve. There does not yet exist a sufficient consensus, a sufficient willingness or commitment for the evolution of effective and far-reaching UN peacekeeping.

Some small progress can be noted. The mandates under which UN peacekeeping forces function are becoming more adequate and allow for somewhat greater effectiveness. UN peacekeeping is a generally popular participation activity. Training for peacekeeping may soon be institutionalized and standardized. There is, however, no indication yet in the UN Committee of 33 on Peacekeeping or elsewhere that major powers are willing to disband their armies and rely on UN peacekeeping as an alternative.

A similar situation exists in the field of peaceful settlement of disputes. In general, the notion of mediated or arbitrated international disputes, with or without UN involvement, is retrograde and in decline. Some small hope for a change in attitude may exist in the examination of UN capabilities for peaceful settlement of disputes through present or improved UN machinery now taking place in the Special Committee on the Charter of the UN and on Strengthening the Role of the Organization. There is, however, no indication that the states of the UN, prizing sovereignty more than security, are prepared at any early date to submit to international procedures as an alternative to their own unilateral actions with regard to dispute settlement any more than with regard to peacekeeping. A small and hopeful straw in the wind may lie in the forthcoming study now being prepared by the UN secretary-general on the relation between disarmament and the means for maintenance of international peace and security; the study may provide at least a self-education exercise for the membership.

In sum, it seems quite clear that unless and until there is a substantial awareness and a high degree of commitment by the international community to the notion of development and implementation of machinery for international peacemaking and peacekeeping, we need not expect, and cannot and will not have, what we and the world so desperately need: an end to the arms race and the achievement of substantial or general and complete disarmament.

The software, contextual problems of the arms race may be described as the "hidden motors" that maintain its life and direction and *result in* the never-ending contest in weaponry. It may safely be said that the symptomatic and visible aspects of the arms race have much deeper and more complex causal aspects which indicate, first of all, that the task before us is more difficult than we have assumed. Second, we must revise the emphases we have up to now placed on hardware negotiations, in favor of a new concentration on the more fundamental "software" problems.

5

Disarmament and International Security—Some New Approaches

William Epstein

It is hardly necessary to point to the failure of the international community to control either the nuclear or conventional arms races. The most striking demonstration of that failure is the fact that annual global military expenditures have quadrupled in the last twenty years from less than $100 billion to more than $400 billion dollars—a significant increase even in *constant* dollar terms—despite the achievement of eight multilateral and twelve bilateral American-Soviet arms-control treaties and agreements. Another startling example is that at the time of the beginning of the SALT negotiations in 1969, the United States had 1,710 strategic missiles and the USSR had about 1,200 missiles, all with single nuclear warheads. Today the United States still has 1,710 of these missiles, with a total of some 4,000 to 5,000 independently targeted nuclear warheads.

The United States has also developed long-range cruise missiles (CMs). These were conceived in the early 1970s as a bargaining chip; first, to help persuade the Soviet Union to enter into the Vladivostok Accord in 1974, fixing the ceiling of 2,400 on all strategic missiles and long-range bombers each for the United States and the Soviet Union, and second, to help make the Vladivostok Accord more acceptable to the U.S. Senate. But, as seems to be the case with such military bargaining chips, once research and development prove their feasibility and effectiveness as weapons, they tend to become immovable blocks.

The development of MIRVs and cruise missiles multiplied greatly the number of strategic warheads, and the accuracy of missiles and their warheads has since been doubling about every four or five years; that is to say, the circular error probable (CEP) has been cut in half every four or five years. The "circular error probable" means 50 percent of the missiles or warheads will land within a circle of given size and fifty percent will land outside. As a result of the remarkable improvement in accuracy, these strategic nuclear weapons

24

are approaching what is known as "absolute accuracy"; that is, they will land within a very short distance of their target—from 50 to less than 500 feet—so that the destruction of the target becomes an absolute certainty.

The development of MIRVs and the rapid improvement in the accuracy of their delivery has tended to undermine such progress as has been made at SALT. There are some students of the problem who say that even if the number of deliverable missiles is reduced by 20 percent a year (from the declining balance) for five years, the effect might be that the killing power of these weapons would not be reduced at all, and it might actually increase.

Other scholars say that, despite the political importance of the SALT negotiations and agreements and their positive effect on the development of détente between the United States and the USSR, they have had little or no importance in terms of disarmament. Except for the ABM treaty, the SALT agreements achieved thus far have put no limit on the qualitative or technological improvement of these weapons. Others say that the SALT negotiations and agreement, although placing numerical limitations on the nuclear arms race, have had the effect of speeding up the qualitative or technological arms race. For example, President Ford said immediately after the Vladivostok Accord that the United States would have to increase the throw weight of its weapons in order to match the Soviet Union. Defense Secretary Schlesinger said that it would be necessary to increase the military budget of the United States and to increase the number of Trident submarines from 10 to 13.

While most scholars and others interested in arms control and disarmament recognize the importance of reaching a SALT II agreement and of having it ratified by the U.S. Senate, a number of them question the value of the agreement if it permits the MARVing of MIRVs (that is, producing MAnoeuverable MIRVs), the production of air-launched, sea-launched, and ground launched cruise missiles, the development and production of MX mobile missiles, the production of Trident submarmines with long-range accurate Trident I and Trident II missiles, and the production of anti-satellite weapons. The development and production of these new highly sophisticated weapons systems could lead both to a proliferation in the numbers of weapons and to enormous difficulties in efforts to limit or eliminate them.

In addition to the strategic, or long-range, nuclear weapons, the technological arms race is proceeding apace with regard to theater, battlefield, and tactical nuclear weapons. Increasingly sophisticated weapons of a variety of sizes, ranges, and purposes are being developed, and some have already been produced and deployed, such as short-range missiles, land mines and artillery shells, the neutron bomb, and Captor mines for use against submarines.

In the field of conventional weapons, too, technology has produced precision-guided munitions (PGMs), remotely piloted vehicles (RPVs), and various automated electronic and "smart" bombs. New "area" weapons have been developed such as cluster bombs and fuel-air-concussion bombs.

The advance of military technology proceeds in many areas and takes advantage of the development of many new electronic devices and sensors. These include radar, infrared lasers, electro-optical devices, computerization, communications, and a variety of homing devices. There is talk at present of producing laser radar called "ladar." In the field of antisubmarine warfare, rapid progress is being made in producing more efficient acoustic and other active and passive sonar devices and sensors. Ultimately, there may be space-based lasers, charged particle beams, or other forms of high-energy rays which might lead to an effective breakthrough in ballistic missile defense, which might erode the viability of the ABM treaty and of mutual nuclear deterrence.

Technological research and development know no limits other than financial restraints. It is worth recalling that in his farewell address President Eisenhower warned not only about the "military-industrial complex" but also about the "scientific-technological elite." Dr. George Heilmeier, then director of the Advanced Research Projects Agency (ARPA) of the U.S. Department of Defense, stated in 1976, "I cannot recall a period in the past decade when so many technological breakthroughs with potential major impact on national security were on the horizon."

Unfortunately, no similar breakthroughs are on the horizon in the field of arms control or disarmament. While military technology is proceeding at a galloping pace, arms control and disarmament negotiations are proceeding at a creeping pace. Prime Minister Nehru of India proposed a ban on the testing of nuclear weapons in 1954. The Partial Test Ban Treaty, banning nuclear weapon tests in the atmosphere, in outer space, and under water, but not underground, was not concluded until 1963; a comprehensive test ban treaty, which would also ban underground tests and peaceful nuclear explosions, has still not been achieved.

The technological arms race creates grave dangers in three respects. First, it tends to upset the military balance, stability, and mutual deterrence. Despite the difficulties of ever achieving a first-strike capability (that is, the ability to disarm the opponent with a first strike so that he cannot retaliate), fears and perceptions generated on one side or the other side of attaining such a capability could erode the reliability of mutual deterrence and lead to a highly dangerous unstable situation.

Second, because of the iron law of technology—that it cannot be monopolized, but will always spread—there will be danger of the horizontal, as well as the vertical, proliferation of both nuclear and conventional weapons. This will greatly increase the danger of an inadvertent war due to accident, miscalculation, human or mechanical breakdowns, or some other form of misadventure. The more weapons proliferate, the more the danger of such a war will multiply.

Third, as indicated previously, the technological arms race makes it much more difficult, if not impossible, to achieve balanced and verifiable agreements to limit and reduce such weapons, let alone to eliminate them entirely. Some consciousness of the seriousness of the threat of advancing technology is beginning to develop, although, I believe, not nearly enough. In regard to the maintenance of international peace and security, the record has not been much better. Since World War II, there have been well over one hundred local or regional wars—fortunately, all of them fought with conventional weapons—with more than twenty-five million dead.

During the time of the League of Nations, there was a great international debate about which came first in the order of priorities—security or disarmament. The debate was never resolved, although it was clear that most countries gave more weight to security. In the early years of the United Nations, the United States and the other Western powers gave clear priority to security over disarmament while the Soviet Union and its allies had the reverse priorities. The issue was finally resolved in the 1961 American-Soviet Joint Statement of Agreed Principles for Disarmament, which was unanimously approved by the General Assembly. The joint statement, in effect, said that progress in disarmament and in international security must go hand in hand, without assigning priority to either.

While this solved the basic issue of priorities, it gave little guidance as to how the agreement was to be implemented. How much disarmament should there be for how much security, or vice versa? What is security, and how can it be measured? What role should be attributed to confidence building, to verification of agreements, to the openness of society, to political détente, and to economic and social conditions? How can collective security be made both feasible and credible? What kind of "international peace force" is necessary to "ensure that the United Nations can effectively deter or suppress any threat or use of arms"? In view of the Great Power veto in the Security Council, would the UN member states have sufficient confidence in an international peace force to undertake serious or far-reaching disarmament? What other security guarantees or assurances might be effective or adequate? All these difficult problems and hard questions are still to be solved.

The various new studies authorized by the General Assembly will undoubtedly help to clarify some of these problems. These studies include: the relationship between disarmament and development; the relationship between disarmament and international security; the study on confidence-building measures; the monitoring of disarmament agreements and strengthening of security through establishment of an international satellite monitoring agency; and the study on nuclear weapons.

In this chapter I propose to discuss four specific aspects of "mechanisms" for improving the prospects for both international security and disarmament.

UNILATERAL INITIATIVES

The arms race has escalated mainly as a result of unilateral and independent measures taken by individual states, often as a response or reaction to unilateral actions taken by another state. It is suggested that converse unilateral initiatives be seriously pursued. Unilateral measures of restraint and arms limitation, and even of reduction of armaments, can be taken on a temporary trial basis in order to stimulate reciprocation and the taking of similar unilateral actions by the other side.

Such unilateral national initiatives can take such forms as moratoria, restraints in the development of new weapons, freezes or reductions of military expenditures, and actual arms reductions. In appropriate cases, such independent steps might be relatively modest ones taken for a temporary trial period in order to stimulate reciprocation by the other party. If there is some comparable response, the initiatives can be enlarged or extended and lead to further reciprocated independent initiatives or to permanent agreements or treaties. One advantage of such approaches is that they can lead to speedy results, avoiding the protracted and painful process of the customary negotiation at arm's length of arms-control agreements, and the need to obtain Senate approval for ratification in the United States.

There have been a number of instances where such unilateral initiatives have produced reciprocation by mutual example—for example, the moratoria on nuclear tests in 1958 and 1959, and the cutbacks in the number of armed forces, military budgets, and the production of fissile material for military purposes in 1963 and 1964. The most successful example was the unilateral decision of the United States in 1969 to renounce the use and possession of all biological weapons and to destroy its stocks (which led to the 1971 treaty to eliminate all biological and toxin weapons). The 1972 interim SALT agreement on offensive weapons, which expired in October 1977, was extended indefinitely by mutual unilateral statements.

Such independent initiatives need not be taken solely to stimulate some comparable reciprocation, although that would be their normal function; there can be instances where they are taken solely for national domestic reasons, as when the United States decided unilaterally not to proceed with developing a binary chemical weapon or the B-1 bomber.

It is obvious that no state would take any unilateral action that would endanger its security. But if each state conducted a serious and thorough review of its military position in order to seek areas where unilateral steps could be taken, it could no doubt find a number of them. Action of this sort could have a major effect in helping to restrain and slow down the arms race, particularly in its qualitative and technological aspects, while accelerating the pace of the negotiations for disarmament agreements.

If the superpowers and other states were to announce several unilateral steps, it would make a profound impact. Such announcements could act as catalysts and stimulate the whole disarmament process. For example, if the United States were to announce the unilateral suspension (for a fixed period of time or, preferably, indefinitely) of underground nuclear testing and the further development and production of the enhanced radiation (neutron) bomb, the long-range cruise missile, and the MX mobile ICBM, that would have a far greater effect than the conditional offer to reduce its strategic missiles by up to 50 percent, provided the USSR does likewise. Such an announcement could be coupled with a call on the Soviet Union to take some comparable unilateral steps, such as suspension of the programs for the SS.16 and SS.20 missiles and the Backfire bomber. It hardly seems likely that the Soviet Union would fail to respond; if it did not make some reciprocal response within a reasonable period of time, the United States could always resume its suspended programs. But the process of international consultations might make this unnecessary.

Because such phrases as "unilateral disarmament" or "unilateral measures" or even "unilateral initiatives" are sometimes mistakenly thought of as meaning that one side totally disarms while the other does not, they are looked upon with suspicion. Various other descriptive names have therefore been invented, such as "reciprocal unilateral restraint" (RUR) or "independent national restraint" (INR). I prefer the name "independent initiatives for reciprocal restraint" (I_2R_2).

A COMPREHENSIVE PROGRAM OF DISARMAMENT

A disarmament program can cover a wide range of measures from a few limited, first-step arms-control and arms-limitation agreements to general and complete disarmament. We have seen that the step-by-step approach, despite some twenty agreements in the last two decades, has failed to slow down the arms race. During the same period, the goal of general and complete disarmament has receded further and further into the future so that nearly all scholars are more or less agreed that it is an ultimate long-range objective that can be attained only with the establishment of a new world order.

The question then arises as to whether some intermediate course might be more successful; that is, whether a comprehensive program for disarmament, consisting of a series of specific measures linked together in one program, or larger "packages" of several measures, might constitute a more fruitful approach.

Some observers of the disarmament negotiations feel that the incremental approach adopted in the past, giving major emphasis to one "non-armament" measure at a time (for example, sea-bed or environment), hinders more rapid progress toward real disarmament. Some also feel that the tendency to pursue issues and negotiations outside of the main negotiating body and in separate, restricted, and somewhat isolated forums for each issue (for example, comprehensive test ban, limitation of conventional arms, anti-satellite warfare, or banning chemical weapons) tends to fragment the disarmament work and to impede the negotiating process. They favor a comprehensive approach in order to negotiate elements of a comprehensive program of general disarmament, and argue that a number of these elements could be negotiated at the same time.

One of the reasons that the incremental approach was doomed to fail is because arms-control negotiations move so much more slowly than do weapons technology and production. It required years of negotiations to achieve each of the limited first-step agreements, and despite commitments to do so, they were not followed by second steps or follow-up agreements. It may be more difficult to arrive at a fair "balance" if it is sought separately for each weapons system, since each country has developed the weapons and military posture it has regarded as necessary for its security in the light of its own geopolitical and strategic requirements. Moreover, each weapon system and each measure of arms control and limitation is interlinked with all the others, and whatever is done about one has an impact on the others. Conversely, it might be easier to arrive at a more acceptable broad balance at lower levels if larger packages of nuclear or conventional disarmament measures, or a mix of both, were attempted.

The experience of the failure to make progress at the Vienna talks on force reductions and of the efforts to control the trade in conventional arms indicates some of the difficulties of dealing with these arms without also taking nuclear weapons into account. And in the nuclear field, some of the problems of achieving a declaration of non-first-use of nuclear weapons and a comprehensive nuclear test ban are made more difficult because of the existing imbalances of conventional forces and arms. It is clear that far-reaching progress cannot be made in either nuclear or conventional disarmament alone without taking the other fully into account. It is possible that a broader mix might also reduce the interservice rivalries that affect the policies of the major powers. In addition, an appropriate mix of elements of comprehensive measures might serve to maintain an arms balance more easily as well as to reinforce specific measures of control and verification. If approached as part of a comprehensive program rather than as isolated small steps, less fear of a small temporary imbalance and greater momentum might also be generated.

In the context of a comprehensive program, it might also be easier to initiate reciprocal or mutual unilateral measures of arms restraint and limitation, which could start or facilitate a process of agreed substantial disarmament.

Reciprocated unilateral initiatives might also result in greater openness and exchange of information and growing confidence and trust. Such unilateral initiatives might be simpler and create less domestic controversy in the national decision-making process than the protracted process of formal negotiations. Experience has shown that they are certainly more rapid and effective.

A comprehensive program of substantial disarmament, with or without unilateral initiatives of arms restraint or limitation, because of its far-reaching nature, might also attract more public interest and the close attention of the highest level of governments and result in more positive feedback than would more limited measures.

The 1978 UN Special Session on Disarmament, in fact, not only elaborated a program of action for disarmament, but also charged the Disarmament Commission (the deliberative forum) to submit recommendations on the elements of a comprehensive program for disarmament to the General Assembly and the Committee on Disarmament (the negotiating body). These are still being refined. They would no doubt also make some recommendations for concurrent progress in the field of international security.

PROPOSALS FOR NEW INSTITUTIONAL AND PROCEDURAL "MECHANISMS"

The Establishment of a New Arms Review Council

This is a novel and somewhat radical longer-term suggestion that may not receive early approval or general endorsement. It is suggested, however, that such a council could be authorized to conduct an annual examination of each state's military policies, military expenditures, and armaments. The council would complement the disarmament review bodies and could conduct its work in a manner similar to that of the UN Decolonization Committee in the past, or to the reviews conducted by the UN Human Rights Commission of the annual reports submitted by governments under the Human Rights Covenant or those by the OECD of the economic policies of member states. If states would have to annually and publicly justify their military policies and budgets in a UN forum, not only their disarmament policies and efforts, this might have a significant restraining influence on the arms race.

Leonard Beaton first put forward a somewhat similar idea some years ago in his book *The Reform of Power*. Other scholars have from time to time made similar proposals. While the idea is indeed novel, it may, if implemented, have an important influence on the military postures of the heavily armed countries. If the idea is pursued, it may in time come to be accepted.

More Openness of Information

Here again, while almost all governments, with important exceptions, approve of the idea in principle, there is noticeable restraint in implementing it. Governments might be asked to furnish annual or periodic reports and information to the United Nations concerning their actions and programs relating to the fields mentioned above, such as armaments, military expenditures, and export and import of arms and nuclear materials and equipment. While some might feel that the furnishing of such information could result in the acquisition of military intelligence and an increase in tensions, many delegates and experts would no doubt feel that the dissemination of such information would probably serve to reduce fears and tensions and to increase confidence. The provision of such information would also, of course, provide the basis for and facilitate the work of an arms review council, if such a council is established.

A number of years ago, after the invention of the atomic bomb, Niels Bohr first suggested that the best way for ensuring that scientific and technological advances would be used for the benefit and not the destruction of humanity was for the great powers to exchange information on their research and development programs and specifically on their military ones. Secretary-General Dag Hammarskjöld took up the idea and officially suggested it in 1958. But in the atmosphere of the Cold War, the idea was dropped. If there is a SALT II agreement and increasing détente between the two superpowers, it might be worth having another look at the idea.

UN System for Regulation of Armaments

Another idea that should be examined is whether the disarmament activities of the UN Security Council and the Military Staff Committee can be reactivated so that they can discharge their responsibilities under Articles 26 and 47 of the UN Charter. Article 26 provides that the Security Council "shall be responsible for formulation, with the assistance of the Military Staff Committee referred to in Article 47, plans to be submitted to the Members of the United Nations for the establishment of a system for the regulation of armaments."

This idea was revived by Finland in the early seventies, and surfaces from time to time. It is in some ways related to the idea of an arms review council.

UN Agency for Arms Control and Disarmament

Another long-range idea concerns the eventual establishment of a new UN agency for arms control and disarmament. Such an agency could coordinate and promote all efforts and negotiations for disarmament and supervise the implementation and verification of all disarmament treaties. It could be brought into a special relationship with the UN, as is the International Atomic Energy Agency (IAEA). Somewhat similar ideas were proposed at the Special Session on Disarmament by the Netherlands and Sri Lanka. While the establishment of such an agency is hardly likely in the near future, the idea merits serious examination.

Creating a Public "Constituency" for Arms Limitation and Disarmament

A number of ideas should be explored in this regard, such as the following:
* Establishing national citizens' advisory committees of scientists, scholars, and representatives of business, labor, and public interest groups to advise the arms-control and disarmament agencies, help formulate national policies and, by being a link to the public, also help to educate and mobilize public opinion
* Establishing an organized dialogue and consultative relationship between national governments and interested nongovernmental organizations, peace research institutes, universities, and other educational bodies on arms-control and disarmament matters
* Having national governments sponsor national and international conferences, symposia, and meetings for the public discussion of issues related to armaments and disarmament
* Having governments establish or sponsor chairs in a number of universities for the study of problems in the field of armaments and disarmament
* Having governments and public interest groups endeavor to attract the interest and participation of journalists and other media persons, and encourage publications in the field and the production of documentary films

The UN Special Session made a number of recommendations for "mobilizing world public opinion on behalf of disarmament." These should all be examined together with the ideas outlined above.

STRENGTHENING INTERNATIONAL SECURITY

The various new "mechanisms" discussed above are concerned mainly with promoting disarmament. They do, however, have a direct relationship to and impact on promoting international peace and security. In fact, the first idea, suggesting the establishment of an arms review council, the third, concerning the possible reactivation of the Military Staff Committee, and the last, on creating a public constituency, all apply in equal measure to enhancing international security and can also be considered and applied in that context.

No nation that feels its security is threatened would be willing to undertake drastic disarmament. The implementation of a program for far-reaching disarmament will require parallel progress toward strengthening the United Nations and its security system, and will require a much more effective system of collective security against war and aggression than now exists, in order that nations may feel that they can safely dispense with the bulk of their military arsenals and systems. To make progress toward this goal, the provision of credible security guarantees will be required as well as the strengthening of the UN's peacemaking, peacekeeping, and enforcement powers. Conversely, balanced reductions in nuclear and conventional armaments to minimum levels of deterrence would enhance the security of all nations and would help to produce a climate of international confidence and trust, which would facilitate the strengthening of the United Nations security system and the full implementation of its enforcement powers under Chapter VII of the UN Charter.

Strengthening the United Nations system and international security is the subject of a vast literature. It was dealt with in detail by Donald Keys in Chapter 4, and I have very little to add to the views expressed by him. Without the mobilization of public opinion and the creation of the necessary political will among both governments and peoples, however, none of the mechanisms is likely to succeed. It is my hope that our discussions might help to clarify the dimensions of the problems involved and that UN studies will point the way and provide some specific guidelines for progress.

Part II
Global Community
Values

6

The Will to Design
a Safe World

Carlos P. Romulo

I have long felt that the problem of the arms race would only yield to a concerted attack by the collected wisdom from all major fields that contribute to the understanding of human nature and world affairs. We have all watched the unabated momentum of the worldwide arms race in its many phases proceed to deprive mankind of the capacity to meet its pressing needs for more years than we would wish to count. We are all aware that the most substantial efforts of nations have been up to now largely unavailing in spite of the best intentions. We are forced, therefore, to look for new understanding of our dilemma and new approaches to the stale and vexing problems linked to our very survival.

The arms race has certainly been less than a "zero-sum game." There are those who will argue that it has provided security in a negative sense and that the balance of military power has prevented catastrophic war. I would stress the word "negative." Fear is not security. Suspicion and uncertainty are not security. If they provide short-term security, they guarantee long-term disaster. I have noted over the years since 1945 two facts with regard to the arms race that have struck me deeply. The first is that it has escalated continuously. The second is that we have looked at the arms race as a mere contest in hardware, which, if mutually scaled down or eventually eliminated, would produce peace and security. Discouragement, frustration, and anxiety have been the fruits of this latter perspective. I believe that the arms race is fundamentally a *product*, not a freestanding phenomenon. I believe it is a product of the *mix* of factors that are operating in the international context at any given time—derived therefore from the *societal context* in which world affairs are conducted.

What are the implications of this view? They are serious and sobering. The first is that a "hardware" approach to disarmament will not suffice. The second is that we must deal as well with the interrelated strands of many historic, social, and psychological factors that form the medium in which the arms race so obviously flourishes. We are forced, therefore, to see our task as

37

more difficult and more vexing than we had thought or hoped. We will need to retool for an interdisciplinary approach. Nothing less will suffice to staunch the flow of the hemorrhaging from the world body politic that the arms race constitutes.

We will necessarily need to focus our efforts on an approach that will *modify* the present societal context, which quite obviously is militating against cessation of the arms race. One particular modification has preoccupied my mind for some years. It concerns the capacities of the world community for "maintenance of international peace and security." I firmly believe that, as I have said on previous occasions, nations cannot and will not disarm into a security deficit or vacuum devoid of alternative means of providing security.

We face a major and historic dilemma. Because of the awesome power we have mustered, sovereign states can no longer provide a reasonable guarantee of safety for their peoples. What goes for security today depends on the holding of entire populations hostage to the terror of nuclear fire. But at the same time, the same states are unwilling or unable to commit equal energy to the design of universally agreed international mechanisms to take the place of the nuclear house of cards that threatens us all. States seem paralyzed in moving toward solutions that would provide for their own survival.

Reflection on this major dilemma suggests that there is as yet insufficient cohesion in the international community to provide the basis and foundation for the necessary security elements of a viable world society. Yet, history appears to demonstrate that true security results from the restraint of violence within an ordered society. Indeed, this is the manner in which human affairs function at all levels except the international level.

A number of years ago, the UN representative of the Netherlands, in a major address to the UN, pointed out that the "pooling of national sovereignty in the common interest" was necessary to survival. It seems to me that this is a most felicitous phrase. It denotes not loss, but gain. It suggests common venture for the mutual good.

The United Nations was founded on the necessity to provide for the "maintenance of international peace and security." The approach taken at that time, however, was an *interim* approach, dependent on the goodwill and collaboration of the permanent members—now all nuclear powers. Such an approach may have been necessary at the time, as the most that was then achievable. No great passage of time was required, however, to illustrate its fatal weaknesses. The approach to providing world security through a concert of major sovereign states essentially failed even from its inception. No alternative approach has taken its place. Thus we are left without security and without the context or setting in which arms limitation, let alone general and complete disarmament, can be entertained as a serious and attainable goal.

Seen in this light, what is required of us as statesmen and scholars is far more than a short-term approach to the immediate exigencies of the arms race.

History is calling upon us to design a world in which we can safely disarm. If we take history as our teacher, it is pointing out that security is a *derivative*—of proper societal organization in all its major elements: shared values, common systems of governance, a process for peaceful settlement of disputes and achievement of justice and equity, *and* the lawfully sanctioned use of force to hold in check socially destructive violence. In a disarmed world, of course, such restraint could be of modest dimensions. In a world armed to the teeth with nuclear weapons and all kinds of massively destructive conventional weapons, restraint of violence is impossible.

In a word, we have to choose the kind of world we want. As intelligent, rational, conscious, and earnestly motivated humans, we as a planetary species can, in my view, doubtless achieve the needed goal. Whether we see the necessity and choose so to do is, of course, quite another matter, and one to which we must direct penetrating attention.

If we look today at the stage of development of security alternatives in the United Nations, the obvious instrument for achievement of our goals, we could easily be discouraged. The rate of evolution of means for peacekeeping and peacemaking is not consonant with the urgent need to dismantle the war machines. Perhaps, then, we as peoples and as nations require to be convinced of the utter necessity to augment alternative measures and pooled approaches to international peace and security. Historically, no other approach commends itself as productive of the sought results.

We can easily list the current forums of the UN in which efforts to progress can be intensified: among others, the Experts' Study on the Relationship between Disarmament and International Security; the long-suffering Committee of 33 on Peacekeeping; and the newer Special Committee on the Charter of the UN and on Strengthening the Role of the Organization, which is presently concentrating on enhancing machinery for peaceful settlement of disputes and maintenance of international peace and security.

We are often instructed that progress is lacking in these areas because of a "lack of will." This is, of course, an unhappy truism. But stated in this manner, it adds nothing to our understanding or to solution of the problem. Lack of will to *what*? If we look at the roots of the problem, we shall discover that the lack of will concerns participation in the structuring and empowering of a global society and a global guidance system. Nations hold back from deepening their commitment to joint efforts and concerted approaches that involve a buildup of effective international machinery. It is in this respect that the "lack of will" is critical and may kill us all. We cannot expect that we have endless time to decide and to act on adequate designs for a control system for planet Earth. A world we once thought was vast, we now experience as a very small planet indeed. The planetary implosion we have wrought with our own hands through the development of science and technology has certain accompanying corollaries and imperatives that have tended up to now to escape us.

The first of these, and the most critical, without which the instruments of Mars will conquer us, is the elaboration and erection of alternative, world-centered modes for maintenance of international peace and security.

7

Four Globalisms

Robert Muller

The fostering of global community values responds to the belief that there is perhaps a roundabout way of introducing a change of values in human behavior that will facilitate disarmament and perhaps render armaments altogether irrelevant in the decades to come. We live in a colossal period of evolutionary change, and during such periods new ideologies, values, philosophies, and perceptions of human fulfillment on our planet might well be the most powerful sinews of change, ultimately more potent than arms, wealth, size, resources, and levels of development. It is a long way, an indirect way, but is definitely worthwhile trying, especially since it is happening before our very eyes.

I have lived the beginnings of this page in the United Nations during the last thirty years, and the best I can do is offer my perceptions of the new global ideology that is emerging from our planet's first universal organization. There is no doubt that the next decades will be very weighty for the future of humanity and that much thought must be given to our fate. There are already numerous people and institutions involved in planetary and long-term evolutionary thinking. Some of them are quite pessimistic. For example, in the United Nations Outer Space Committee, the views of astrophysicists were sought on the question of life in the universe, and we were told that once a living species has reached our level of development, two fundamental questions arise: Will the species be able to manage properly its planet? Will it be able to solve its intergroup relations or social problems?

Sir Fred Hoyle, the astronomer, holds the view that human intelligence was the compensation for a lack in physical strength and that this intelligence will now cause our destruction. He does not give us even 10,000 years of survival, a mere speck of time in evolution. But there are also other long-term thinkers who are, on the contrary, refreshingly optimistic. Teilhard de Chardin, the archaeologist and theologian, after a lifetime of study of the past of our planet and of the human species, concluded that humanity would enter a new age of evolution and metamorphose itself into a higher, peaceful, more responsible, superconscious and spiritual global species. Vernadsky, the biologist who invented the concept of the biosphere, shared these views. We are indeed witnesses at this moment of a profound biological transformation of humanity, a passage from protohumans to metahumans. We are truly being transformed into a planetary species with a global brain and nervous system and the beginnings of a global heart. Planetary perceptions and warnings are taking place all the time. We can feel them down to the individual. We react to them and we begin to change our behavior. Global censuses, inventories, diagnoses, thinking, recommendations, plans, and actions are flourishing in a multitude of world meetings and institutions, a good part of them under the United Nations umbrella. At this particular exciting juncture of our planet's history, anyone who believes in the future of humanity[1] has the opportunity to help develop four categories of new global community values: globalism in space, globalism in time, global institutions, and global education.

GLOBALISM IN SPACE

From my close association with the work of the thirty-two United Nations specialized agencies and world programs, it is very clear that humanity has undergone a phenomenal mutation in its knowledge of the universe. We have multiplied the capacities of our inherited "natural" senses (such as the visual, auditive, and cerebral) by the millions of times and, as a result, especially during the last thirty years, have been able to penetrate far into the infinitely large and the infinitely small. It suffices to visit an astronomic observatory and an atomic bubble chamber to see how our species has been able to "grow" and "sharpen" its eyes and brain into both the vastness and the smallness of the universe. And this has happened in every direction.

Ours is a very tiny planet in the heavens. At a distance of a few hundred thousand miles away in space, it disappears from sight. But on this little planet dwells a species that is capable of elevating itself into the infinitely large, of penetrating into the infinitely small, and of trying to understand everything near and far in the universe, including itself. The result has been a truly extraordinary explosion of knowledge and of global views of the space in which we live.

What has happened is that the astrophysicists have given us a global view of the universe, the outer space specialists a global view of outer space, the solar experts a global view of our relations with the sun, the biologists a global view of the biosphere, the hydrologists a global view of the world's water, and so on and so forth. As a matter of fact, it seems that we are living in a universe of spheres within spheres. Outer space could well be called the outer sphere. Within the biosphere there is the atmosphere, the ozonosphere, the troposphere. The Earth's crust is called the lithosphere, the world's waters are called the hydrosphere, and so on down to the atom, which has the shape of a tiny solar system. All these layers and spheres cut across our traditional, antiquated, separatist political thinking and structures. These global views of the world have all found their way to the United Nations where they have been sharpened in a series of resounding world conferences and reverberated to all governments and peoples of this planet: conferences on outer space, the biosphere, the environment, the seas and oceans, the deserts, the world's water, the world's climate, down to the arable layer of the earth's crust, underground water and mineral resources, geothermal energy, microbiology, and the atom. On nearly every single aspect of our physical world, we possess now a global view. This is a tremendous advance in evolution. It has rallied practically all scientists and people who are dealing with these issues; they have become globalists. Any scientist who is dealing with a global subject considers his subject to be more important than the political divisions of the planet. Two of my children are scientists; one in nutrition, the other in oceanography. They do not care very much about the national subdivisions of planet Earth: one sees the seas and oceans as a global reality teeming with life and exciting mysteries; the other sees the nutrition of the human person as a global problem concerning the entire humanity. The unity of science is a great advance, a new paradigm that will sooner or later force politicians down on their knees and make them change their minds. At the United Nations' world conferences, national delegates are already subjected to these changes, and they in turn are changing the outlook of their governments, especially when they return home as ministers of so-called foreign affairs.

The new view of our place in space is accompanied by a new view of our species as a whole. We have never been perceived by political men as a totality. Only great prophets, visionaries, and philosophers have always seen us as an entity. For holding this simple, fundamental, and striking truth, they were crucified, locked up, or scoffed at as "naive" and as fools. Of late, this has changed. For the first time in history, in humanity's global institutions, the human species has been inventorized, classified, taken stock of, and studied from every possible angle. For the first time since the Romans, censuses have been taken of the whole human realm; we now know how many we are, our composition by sex, our age structure, our dynamics of change, our nutritional levels, literacy, employment, state of health, and other factors. The world population conference took stock of humanity as a whole. UNICEF and the International Year of the Child are concerned with children. The World Conference on Youth dealt with the young. A World conference on the elderly will be held in 1982. The cause for all this was not logical neatness or "vision," but the dire necessity to look at our new pressing global problems. For example, the problem of aging is of a global nature because hundreds of millions of elderly people will be added to this planet during the next decades. Thus, one after the other, we mark tremendous advances in globalism. Never before in the entire evolution of this planet has there been a single global conference organized by one of the living species.

On one aspect of human globalism we are still lagging considerably behind, namely, group relations. Humans are studied quantitatively, statistically, and scientifically; they can be counted, measured, classified and analyzed. But when it comes to the functioning of the human society in terms of groups, one does not yet find much globalism. In this realm, we have made little progress. There are not any true global social sciences, excepting perhaps Margaret Mead's global anthropology. There is no worldwide global psychology, worldwide sociology, world philosophy. The group, the culture, the past, the history, the language, the territory still stand potently in the way of needed new global community values. The supreme global value of the survival and fulfillment of the human species has not yet been admitted. Social sciences, as distinct from physical sciences, have not yet outgrown their compartmentalized historical past. They keep away from global values, which might impair their current beliefs and positions. This is very serious. It has led, among other things, to the failure of the United Nations in political relations. Indeed, all the United Nations could do during the last thirty years was to build bridges between groups: between nations, races, sexes, ages, the poor and the rich, East and West, and nations and transnational corporations. As U Thant said, "The greatest value of the United Nations in a world of group aspirations and conflicts is to build bridges." This is why he called his memoirs *The View from the Bridge*.

As regards the social cosmos, universities, academies, and individual thinkers have a greater freedom than the United Nations. Hence, the United Nations University, the Peace University in Costa Rica, and the proposed United States Peace Academy are places where the world's finest minds can begin to develop a global philosophy for the human family seeking its way on a limited but miraculous planet. In the United Nations we cannot go that far and fast. For the time being, we are merely bridge builders between potentially conflicting groups who each still cling to the belief that they are the greatest and the holders of the ultimate truth. What one sees today in the United Nations is somewhat similar to what occurred between the religions. All nations and religions are pursuing in the end the same objective: the good and happiness of people; hence, the sudden sprouting of ecumenism, globalism, and universalism. This is an immense step forward. From now on, the affairs of this planet will never be the same.

In short, what stands out is the staggering progress of the scientific and technological knowledge of our planet and of the universe, from the infinitely large to the infinitely small. This has produced an astonishingly complex, mysterious, and tremendously beautiful image of the place of our planet and of its life forms in the universe. Our knowledge has spread in every possible direction, an event tantamount to a phenomenal transcendence of a species— our species—on one of the lucky life-endowed planets in the universe.

Alas, when it comes to the human cosmos, almost everything remains to be done. Our planetary cathedral is not yet occupied by a reverent, grateful, transcendent, and united community of peoples, but by unruly groups of immature, conflicting children.

GLOBALISM IN TIME

Good progress has also been made of late in what I would call globalism in time. When I was a young man, human thought had a very short time dimension. Five-year economic planning was a rare exception to be found only in the socialist countries. Not so long ago, in the seventeenth century, Bishop Ussher estimated that the Earth was created in 4004 B.C.! Today our planet is known to be 4.5 billion years old, and paleontology and archaeology have made immense strides. Futurology is a much more recent discipline, a true milestone in evolution. Today there is not a government that does not think or plan at least twenty or thirty years ahead. In the United Nations, planning reaches at least to the year 2000, if not beyond, as is the case for demography and climatology. The important fact is that humanity has reached a point in evolution when it is compelled to perceive and include in its thinking an ever-larger segment of the totality of time allotted to our planet.

This comes in addition to our species' progress toward comprehension of the total physical reality. Astrophysicists tell us that the rest of our planetary time is from six to eight billion years. Climatologists tell us that our next preoccupation will be the recurrence of an ice age; hence, the decision of the United Nations to convene a world climate conference to review the scientific knowledge gathered so far. More immediately, when the Club of Rome came out with its report on the limits of growth, it created a vast concern and discussion all around the world, because every human being felt that it touched upon a very timely and sensitive issue dealing with our future. As a result, futurology and the increase in the time dimension of scientific, governmental, and world thinking has revealed the global interdependence of our species in time.

The more we see the world in the long run, the more we must revise our values so as not to endanger our planet and to ensure our survival on it. This is why many long-term thinkers believe that our foolishness in keeping thousands of nuclear weapons in the air, land, and sea environments are proof that human "intelligence" is incapable of survival and will lead to its self-destruction. Indeed, it is difficult to visualize how we could maintain the present number of atomic weapons for centuries or for thousands of years, and further increase their number and deadliness, without the risk, sooner or later, of an accident and nuclear holocaust. We can therefore no longer admire countries who submit the world to such a risk. In the age of global interdependence, a nation's greatness must be measured by its peacefulness and contribution to human civilization, not by its arsenals.

I would like here to address an appeal to the political and social sciences. While most exact sciences are geared to the future and fascinated by it (for example, astrophysics, space science, electronics, engineering, nuclear science, and medicine), the social sciences again are falling far behind. They relish dwelling in the past or at best in the present. There is virtually no theology, philosophy, anthropology, sociology, or political science of the future. Millions of pages are written every year on innumerable minute facts of the present and the past, which will quickly fall into oblivion, while little is being published on the society of the future. Generations to come will judge very harshly today's social scientists for their lack of breadth and vision. They will rightly ask the social sciences why they were so blind, so unimaginative, and so irresponsible toward the future of human civilization. I could often cry or explode when I see the amount of futile, useless works produced by the current social sciences. How can they be so impermeable to what is happening on this planet?

GLOBAL INSTITUTIONS

A third area of hope is the institutional one. Our planetary evolution has been marked during the last thirty years by a flourishing of global institutions. The United Nations itself is very different from what it was at its birth. I would have never dreamed in 1948, when I joined the UN, that today we would have thirty-two specialized agencies and world programs covering practically every global aspect of the human condition.

In addition, there are many other mushrooming, growing, and spreading international and transnational entities, such as corporations, nongovernmental organizations, transnational professions, and trade unions. There are tens of thousands of them today, as distinct from a mere handful at the beginning of this century. They exercise a deep role in kneading, transforming, and globalizing the world. Suffice it to mention that for the first time in history, a professional association, the International Pilots' Association, was able to force the United Nations Security Council to meet on one of their problems: hijacking. A completely different and new world view is in the making. Something has struck me very much regarding the institutional phenomenon: international entities have become very vital instruments of group learning. The United Nations system is, more than anything else, a great international school for nations. There, they see each other collectively, they begin to better understand each other, to take inventory of our planetary conditions, to signal back home global messages and warnings, to manage the planet in common, and progressively develop a philosophy and vision of what human destiny should be on our globe. We are right in the midst of an evolutionary phase that one might call "consensus in diversity." In this regard, I would like to mention the famous exchange of views between Einstein and Freud in 1932, which seems to be very relevant to this subject.

Einstein, as many scientists today, could not understand why his discoveries were being turned into instruments of death and why we were living on a planet armed to its teeth. All his personal crusades, plans, and efforts at disarmament having failed, he turned to Freud and asked if the psychologists had possibly an answer to the problem. Freud replied that humans were basically torn between two tendencies, aggression and love. Love was the main psychological means to hold a group together. He recommended, therefore, that by every possible means, "ties of sentiment" should be developed between nations in order to assert for the first time humanity as the supreme group. He considered the League of Nations an unprecedented experiment in this direction and appealed to all peoples to support it. Thus, he wrote:

We should be taking a very shortsighted view of the League of Nations were we to ignore the fact that here is an experiment the like of which has rarely—never before, perhaps, on such a scale—been attempted in the course of history. It is an attempt to acquire the authority (in other words, coercive influence), which hitherto reposed exclusively in the possession of power, by calling into play certain idealistic attitudes of mind," including "ties of sentiment" or "identifications" between the members of the group as opposed to violent compulsion.[2]

The League of Nations failed, but what Freud said in 1932 still holds true today. Therefore, the United Nations and the new international institutions are much more vital than we all think. They are part of a new, deep-seated evolutionary process. They exercise a novel global biological function of the human species. They are the place where fears, warnings, learning, understanding, adaptations, and ties of sentiment are developed. They will be considered someday as one of the great paradigms of a new epoch. This is why I will never cease to speak, to plead, to write, and to ask for the support of these entities that are so vital for the survival and further evolution of the human race.

Thus, the dream of many prophets and visionaries is at long last becoming true. For the first time ever on this planet, we are blessed with universal organization. Yet it seems that many people do not even take notice of it. It is in every person's interest to support the world entities and organizations. It is our duty to properly inform the public, which is practically blanked out about the far-reaching, epoch-making work of the United Nations and its agencies. It is the duty of governments to give adequate moral, political, financial, and informational support to these organizations. When I was director of the UN budget, I once asked that a comparative study be made of the growth of the United Nations budget and of national budgets. Many governments considered this to be a major heresy! The need to better inform the public brings me to the last and perhaps most important area where globalism must be developed: namely, education.

GLOBAL EDUCATION

In the long run, only the right global education will be our salvation on this planet. This was the view of U Thant, a former teacher, who often said that only the future generations could be counted on to manage this planet in peace, justice, and happiness for all. This is why he supported so strongly the international schools and proposed the creation of a United Nations University. He was absolutely right. Children are born with more or less the same senses into the world. But very soon they are "wired in" by a culture, a religion, an ideology, a nation. There is only one thing with which they are never really wired in: their membership in the entire human family. It is inconceivable to me that, after having discovered our global place in the universe, the global aspects of our planet, and our global destiny in time, we should not also teach someday to our children about the global human race. Not to do so would be an evolutionary aberration. The present state of education throughout the world lags dangerously behind natural and man-made global, interdependent realities. It needs urgent updating. If an interplanetary inspection team were to visit our planet, it would certainly point at the lack of proper world education as one of our greatest and most dangerous deficiencies. They would place emphasis on a rewiring of human beings in order to give us an objective view of the planet on which we live and of our human family. There is need for a change of the curricula, not only in primary schools, but also at the academic level. I have not found so far one single "university" on this planet that would have a truly "universal" view. And I would not send my children to any of the existing faculties of international affairs, which are usually aeons away from what is known in the United Nations and its agencies about the true conditions of our planet and of its people. Perhaps, to conclude, the best illustration in this regard is the following parable or "cri du coeur" written by an educator at the Kettering Foundation:

A Parable

Once upon a time there was a class,
and the students expressed disapproval of their teacher.
Why should they be concerned with
global interdependency, global problems
and what others of the world were thinking, feeling and doing?
And the teacher said she had a dream in which she
saw one of her students fifty years from today.
The student was angry and said,
"Why did I learn so much detail about the past
and the administration of my country
and so little about the world?"
He was angry because no one told him
that as an adult he would be faced

almost daily with problems of a
global interdependent nature, be they
problems of peace, security, quality
of life, food, inflation, or scarcity
of natural resources.
The angry student found he was the
victim as well as the beneficiary.
"Why was I not warned? Why was
I not better educated? Why
did my teachers not tell me about
the problems and help me understand
I was a member of an interdependent
human race?"
With even greater anger the student shouted,
"You helped me extend my hands with incredible machines,
my eyes with telescopes and microscopes,
my ears with telephones, radios, and sonar,
my brain with computers,
but you did not help me extend
my heart, love, concern
to the entire human family.
You, teacher, gave me half a loaf."

Jon Rye Kinghorn

NOTES

1. This basic option has led Norman Cousins to divide humanity, not into East and West, North and South, black and white, rich and poor, but into pessimists and optimists, namely those who believe and those who do not believe in the progress of the human race. See his Preface to my book, *Most Of All, They Taught Me Happiness* (Doubleday, 1978).

2. Otto Nathan and Heinz Norden, eds., *Einstein on Peace* (New York: Schocken Books, 1968), p. 196.

8

Discussion

The following discussion took place in the course of the symposium held in Conference Room 7 of the United Nations.

Geoffrey Pearson: I should be in another room here voting on disarmament resolutions rather than talking with you about disarmament. In fact, the issue there right at the moment is whether to authorize the UN to produce a film on war, which would cost something like $200,000 or a little more, and which yesterday took three hours of discussion, after which the matter was adjourned. I won't structure my little talk around the issue of that film, although it somehow and in some ways epitomizes some of the problems that we are dealing with. In any event, it was not agreed to yesterday and I think it will be today, but there were a number of objections, a lot of them under the surface. Those of us who could follow the nuances could see that there were some real issues involved about whether such a film, despite its very modest cost, would be something that the UN should do.

I am a professional diplomat and, for my sins, a disarmer, and I have to engage in a great deal of that whatever you want to call it—double talk perhaps, or role playing to which you were referring—and I am very conscious of the gap or difference between the role one plays as an official or government representative and one's own values, assuming one knows what they are. I think you made an extremely important point about whether one does know, whether most of us do know what we are. Perhaps it is too difficult for us, too time consuming, too dangerous for us to look at that—especially for officials, I may say. And that, of course, is why diplomats were invented, especially in order to avoid values so that you have a code of protocol and procedures and behavior which enable you to communicate with each other in a language—I don't mean a spoken language, but in the language of behavior, which is understood on all sides and therefore facilitates communication without raising the question of values.

There is something to be said for that, and perhaps something to be looked at in terms of the future software of the global society and global values; something to be looked at in terms of the dangers of going in a different direction. At least, we should ask ourselves if we are ready for it yet.

I wanted to say just a few words about the situation that my country is in. I am Canadian, and I am glad to be here as a Canadian because the Canadians speak the same language—in the same sense I meant before—as Americans.

But we sometimes feel ourselves to be in a different kind of environment when we come here. This is particularly true of disarmament, I think, or at least I'll make it true for today.

Most of the writing on disarmament and arms control and international relations comes to us from the United States. And I think this is true whether one is a Canadian, an Englishman, a Frenchman, or a German. This is generally true. And the problems raised in this literature are very much the problems of the United States as a superpower; of the United States as a power with weapons that the rest of us simply don't have and know very little about, and therefore do not face us with the same kinds of dilemmas, if you like. And the explanations for this situation, naturally, are given in terms of the American situation.

I was reading Professor Singer's piece that was circulated to us before we came here, I think written in 1958. It is very stimulating still today, still very appropriate and it must rather depress you because it was written more than twenty years ago and I don't think you can change a word of it today. Oh, you might not be so optimistic at the end. But look at the problems he raised which are said to lead to war: political disputes—that's the most common, political tensions, and disputes. We don't have any in Canada. We have some problems with our neighbor, but they aren't serious. They certainly don't lead to mobilization; at least, they haven't for a long time. Action-reaction—the old explanation that what one power does, the other power is led to do, and so on in the escalation process—certainly doesn't apply to us in terms of our perceptions of the world, although it does in the sense that we are members of an alliance. The military-industrial complex? We don't have one. We have one of the smallest armies in the world compared to our wealth: not even 80,000 people, and that is for all three services. Our industrial complex in terms of armaments is minuscule. We produce some aircraft and we try to sell some spare parts to the United States, but the military-industrial complex is not a factor in my country.

One often explains the arms race in terms of the technological imperative: how the scientists, laboratory technicians, or engineers simply go on inventing new things because that is what they do; if they can draw it, they can produce it. Well again, this is more like a worldwide phenomenon, but it doesn't apply to us because we don't have an arms industry in that sense.

The last explanation one might use—and I am being very arbitrary here, not trying to be scholarly—is the question of national status and national pride. That is very true of our country. I think it is probably true of any country. I would give it, therefore, very high marks in terms of what leads to the creation of armed forces, the perpetuation of armed forces, and the buildup of weapons and armaments. After all, we do have armed forces. They are armed, and they look for the best equipment. We are in the market at the moment for one-hundred and twenty or so fighter aircraft at a very high cost, a couple of billion dollars, I think. And the reason we do that is not really for the defense of our country—although roles will be invented—but because we have an air force. We do have an air force, so we have got to give it something to do. And we have got to have an air force, because we are an important country; that's part of our perception of ourselves. And we belong to an alliance. We must contribute to that alliance. Therefore, we must do our share. If that means buying important and sophisticated weapons, we will do that.

I might point to a couple of other factors which I think are important in Canadian thought on this subject. In addition to the question of status, why do we feel that we need to belong to an alliance called NATO, that we agree with concepts such as deterrence? By the way, that whole question seems to me to require greater thought and more explanation because deeply held both by governments and by peoples is the concept of deterrence—that there is someone out there who looks like he's going to, or has the capacity to, threaten you, and that you must deter him.

This concept for us had been deeply imbedded in our consciousness, along with that of other Western countries, by the Second World War and by the experience of the 1930s. Canadians were called up on day one of the war in 1939 because of our relations with Britain and because Canadians assumed that since Britain was at war, then we should be. And we weren't prepared; we had nothing. In fact, I think our armed forces were then 25,000. At the end of the war we were the third or fourth most important military power in the world after the defeat of Germany and Japan. Thus the idea of deterrence. If you wish to prevent war, arm. This idea was deeply held by the politicians of Canada and, I think, of most countries after the war, and it is still very much alive. One cannot, it seems to me, cope with the whole problem of disarmament until one deals with this concept and deals with it in a way that is convincing both to officials and to the general public. It leads directly to alliance commitments. That is why we are a member of an alliance. That is why I suspect we will continue to be. And once you are a member of an alliance, then this whole business of role playing, of doing our part, of contributing our share, becomes extremely important.

Perhaps I could turn briefly from a discussion of Canada to an order of ideas which I have always found puzzling: the role of public opinion. Professor Singer argues in his piece that the elite is able, in effect, to control public opinion or manipulate it in some way; that public opinion isn't really all that important, at least in Western countries. I think that it's probably true to some extent, although I would add that it seems to me that the reason that a country like mine or a country like the United States is able to maintain armed forces prepared to fight a major war is the existence of a public opinion which by and large approves. This is true of Canada, even though we have no history of conflict in the same way that Europeans do. One European once told me, after he came to Canada from Czechoslovakia, that he was astonished by the fact that Canadians tended to question the need for defense spending. He said: "In Europe we simply assume that the world is insecure, that it has been insecure for centuries. No one questions the fact that you need armed forces. This is the first country that I have come to where this question was ever raised."

If it is raised, however, it's not raised or dealt with or pursued for very long. In general, as soon as you get below a certain level of arms, that is, as soon as you begin to question the fact that we should contribute to the alliance in some measurable way which we can defend, then public opinion rapidly turns against the government.

I mentioned here also the dangers of saying to people things which seem to them to be extreme, because I think the ordinary man is probably fairly astute in his perception of what people say to him. A solution such as, "Well, the only way to change this is to have a world government" is one thing that people sometimes say. My experience is that the ordinary person simply doesn't listen as soon as you finish saying that, because it means nothing to him. Even if he thinks it is a good idea, it is a long way off. Most people don't think it is a good idea. In Canada, we are over-governed.

Then there are other ways of trying to deal with this subject. Some of us outside of government and inside in the academic community or in world disarmament sometimes point to solutions which are either too absolute or which are too idealistic or too arbitrary a practice which seems to me hardly to amount to sensible policymaking. But, obviously, one does not want to discourage interest and enthusiasm for the subject.

I think the idea which the president of France discussed at the Special Session on Disarmament—called *"sur àrmament"*—the notion of over-armament—is a good one to put forward because I think what we are really dealing with is overkill, fantastic amounts of capability and weapons which the ordinary man, or public opinion, if you like, *does* understand. It's no good telling him that he shouldn't have a gun, if he feels he is threatened. But if you tell him that he doesn't need a howitzer, perhaps he will respond. Finally, in this area of public opinion, I think it is important, very important, to distinguish between the short term and the long term. And this, I think, relates a bit to the idea of *sur àrmament*, over-armament, in the sense that, in the short term, we are facing very clear and present dangers—and by the "short term" I mean over the next ten or fifteen years—of blowing ourselves up. Nuclear proliferation in both senses, horizontal and vertical, it seems to me, will be the greatest threat that we face to the end of the century in terms of our future as human beings, not because anyone intends nuclear war, but because of the dangers of accidents and so on. It seems to me that these are the problems that we should be concentrating on over the next few years.

In the long term, obviously, one wants to get something quite different, some kind of stable or minimum deterrence, what countries need to defend themselves to keep the internal order, and so on. But to talk too much about those longer-term problems—(this is my own view, and I may be quite wrong)—over the next few years is probably to misplace our priorities. Perhaps what we really have to do is to concentrate on the overriding and overwhelming problems of nuclear spread.

Finally, a word on the role of the UN. Again, short term and long term, I think. The only solution David Singer could see more than twenty years ago was to give the UN powers that would enable countries to feel secure, so that even if they were disarmed, they would know that there was some organization, supra-national organization, which was able to perform the role of the policeman in the world. This is clearly not going to be the case. It is clearly not going to be the case in the next twenty years. It is not going to be the case, I would have thought, in the next fifty years. But this is just a matter of anyone's guess.

In the short term, what the UN is going to be able to do is gradually improve its capacities to render help in conflict situations such as the Middle East. That is a very important thing, and we should do all we can to help it. But goodness, it's like pushing the largest boulder uphill. We haven't gotten very far in the last twenty years. Singer was writing just after Suez. We now have a lot of experience at peacekeeping. The political problems, the political suspicions, the political difficulties are just as great if not greater. They must have something to do with these values you were talking about. But it has more to do, I think, with questions involving status, sovereignty, and national pride. I'll end up by saying something about why I think that is true.

Second, on the UN and international law, I think gradually the UN can give us a sense that there are rules that are universal, even though they are not laws but are declarations, procedures, and rules.

Third, I think that in the short term the UN can help persuade the founders, the fifty-one countries that signed the charter, that the instrument they forged needs revision; that there are now one-hundred other countries, and that the world has changed and we have got to do something about that instrument we invented. In the long term, we have to reform that whole structure. It's no good talking about changing the voting rights now. But in the longer term we have to reform it, and we have to gradually transfer to the UN, in the way that Professor Singer was talking about, greater and greater amounts of authority which it can gradually take on and exercise.

My conclusion relates to what I think are major impediments to disarmament at the present time. I've just written down three. One is that the world is in a state of revolution that I think is unique in our history. For one thing, we now have a global community which is virtually free—free in the sense that there are no empires, or very few, assuming that the Soviet Union and a few other countries are countries rather than empires. But in a more general sense, we have a world of one-hundred and fifty to one-hundred and sixty states, which is a unique and probably stable phenomenon—stable in the sense that it won't get much larger and it's very doubtful that we will let it get much smaller. This world of one-hundred and sixty or more states needs a little more time to shake down. These new states, ten years old, twenty years old, are simply not going to take from us, in that short time or over the next five years, lessons on how to conduct themselves, when we, the older states, have clearly not learned them ourselves—particularly in this area of disarmament. One of the most sensitive issues at the Assembly is this whole question of arms transfer. And it is not very easy for any of us in the West to suggest that we should cut back on the export of arms to new states or to poor states because they are going to mismanage them, or they don't know what to do with them, or they will kill each other, and so on. This is a notion which they do not accept very gracefully and they do not support.

The second major impediment, and I don't put these in any particular order, is technology. I think people are probably right about this: that the rate of technological development and inventiveness is almost out of control. I have no answers to that. I don't know what the answer is.

Third, and perhaps paradoxically related to the first, is the spread of education and of communications around the world; rapid communications. Whereas before you were dealing with, shall we say, sinful elites, you are now dealing with middle classes, educated classes in almost every country. Certainly, in the short term and from my observation, this does not lead to any greater inclination to be sensible about world politics, but quite the reverse. What it leads to is greater bellicosity, greater aggressiveness. It makes it easier for the communications media, the press, and so on to manipulate opinion, and I think probably we are in the stage where this is going to be true for some time longer.

Ervin Laszlo: As we continue on this level of extremely thought provoking ideas, it reminds me, if I can take just one moment, of a conference we had on the world system in 1973 to which Margaret Mead came. We had what appeared to be a disagreement, which took a half hour to clear up. It was on the following point, which is very close to the remarks that Robert Muller made: Is the world society as a whole a self-regulative system, or is it not? I, using biological, social, and general evolution evidence, said that it is bound to be a self-regulative system. Sooner or later it will find its new balance on the global level. Margaret Mead said, "No, there is no record in human history that it has regulated itself. It needs some conscious planning and intervention in this system."

It turned out that the crux of the matter was that we often tend to forget that *our* ideas, our initiatives, are part of this system which we are talking about. If we take ourselves into account, then we find in some instances—such as these and such as that conference in 1973—that there is a birth of that kind of consciousness about which Robert Muller was talking. You mention at one time that in certain respects the UN cannot go further, while we are now at the

UN, we are in these discussions going further, and we are a part of this system. And perhaps this is how things have to grow, here and there, by attempting to bring about this kind of regulation in the system. In that sense, I share the optimism of Robert Muller if he continues being an element in the system rather than sitting back on the outside and saying, "Well, it runs to its doom by itself." But if he works with it, possibly he can change its course and bring about the kinds of ideas that we have been discussing today.

David Singer: One of the reasons that I decided to participate in this conference is that the co-chairmen, if you will, represent my two most highly valued values: Donald Keys representing the world citizen, planetary citizen orientation and certainly a value that I assume that most of us assign very high priority to; and Ervin Laszlo being one of the key figures in the general systems movement. It has always seemed to me—and I was particularly reinforced in this as I listened to Robert Muller—that the general systems approach to the problem of world peace and to the more specific problem of world disarmament offered more promise than virtually any other approach. This is partly because we are always reminded, using a general systems orientation, how fantastically interdependent not only sectors of societies and strata of societies are, and how interdependent we are among our social and our political, material, and technological activities, but also because of the theme that has come up increasingly in the futuristic work: that there are all kinds of non-trivial, unanticipated consequences of our actions.

Now, I would certainly be the last one in this room to suggest that futurology is a science. As a matter of fact, I think I would take second place to nobody in my disdain for the methodology that futurologists use. My impression from reading most of this literature is that in the futurology literature we are being treated to the phenomenon of human beings believing that if they slap different labels to their perceptions of reality, they have somehow or other helped diagnose the problem, clarified the analytical characteristics, and begun to lay out some sort of solutions.

I am not only bored by futurology; I am terrified by it. Muller has suggested that the curriculum in most universities around the world is pretty bad, and I think that is an understatement. I am glad you mentioned Harvard and, I think, Princeton, but even good universities such as the University of Michigan have problems. The reason, it seems to me, is that neither the planetary view nor the general systems view has found its way into the curriculum.

Let me draw on the general systems idea in more detail. One of the key notions in the general systems perspective is that of "steersmenship," the search for self-amplifying and self-correcting mechanisms. There is a literature known as cybernetics, and we employ the basic principles of cybernetics very skillfully, as you reminded us, in the solution of a tremendously varied, complex, and difficult set of physical, mechanical, engineering, and biological problems. But I cannot find much evidence that we apply the cybernetic principle to the analysis of the solution of social problems. To put it more generally, it is very difficult to find much evidence that the scientific method as an intellectual style, as a human value, is brought to bear on the solution of social problems. And this is particularly true in the field of world peace and in the field of world disarmament.

I detect in the three speakers so far a charming sense of patience. The more I listened to all three of you, the more impatient and nervous and anxious I became because, as an historian whose basic research is on the correlates of international warfare since the congress of Vienna, one of the things that strikes me is the frequency with which each of the 99 major international wars and the 103 major civil wars since the congress of Vienna, but particularly the international wars, surprised the people who ended up fighting and dying in them. There were those who were the pessimists, and then there were those who were the optimists. The optimists almost always carried the day. The optimists were always the ones who said, "What you need is a little more of this. What we need is a little more time. What you have to do is increase your preparedness here. What you have to do is strengthen this particular defensive salient." There were always people who had one or another quick fix, and these people were always wrong.

It seems to me that if we began to bring the cybernetic perspective and the scientific mode to bear on what have been the conditions that differentiated between war and non-war outcomes, let us say in military confrontations in the last 160 years, we might begin to make some interesting discoveries. At this moment I am being rather autobiographical, because I have devoted virtually all of my research time in the last ten years to precisely this question. The findings to date are far from conclusive. But one of the findings that I think I can mention right off is that in no decade since the Napoleonic Wars has there been fewer than four major international wars, and a typical decade has had six or seven—and that includes, of course, this very decade.

There are some encouraging trends. For example, since World War I, the typical decade has seen a very slight decline in the number of major power wars, but not in the number of international wars, and the period since World War II has seen a very slight decline in the number of military confrontations or crises involving major powers. Now you could look at these things and say "Ah, we do have the kind of time that is implied in some of the earlier comments. What we need is patience coupled with bridge building coupled with skillful diplomacy." My strong sense is that patience is not what we need; skillful diplomacy is almost a contradiction in terms, and all of the bridge building that we have been engaging in is bridge building that we have seen go on over and over, and it is not a longitudinal, upward secular trend; it is cyclical. Bridge building goes along for a while, then you have your conflagration.

For example, one of my studies dramatically illustrates that there is no correlation between the number or size or function of international organization in the international system in a given year and the amount of war that begins in the next year. But, lo and behold, there is a very strong positive correlation between the amount of war that ended in a given year and the amount of new international organization that gets constructed in the next five years. That is, we keep building these bridges in the hope that somehow or other they are going to work. They have not worked in the past, and my forecast is that they are not going to work in the future. They are going to be demolished.

Let me offer a brief theoretical perspective here in which values become an important catalytic ingredient. People have been arguing that the way to break out of the arms races of the present and the past or those that might occur in the future is through, for example, consciousness-raising and enhancing global values. I would like to argue that there is no way to enhance global values in those nations which are engaged in the preparedness program. It flies in the face of everything that psychologists, sociologists, and political scientists have discovered, because it somehow assumes that as nations allocate resources to military preparedness, nothing else happens in the society. Bear in mind that general publics, no matter how politically indifferent and how deeply addicted they are to one or other of the opiates of the masses, whether it is religion, television comedy, or football, somehow accept the idea that there is some need to allocate resources to military preparedness; there is some need to take our sons and brothers and husbands; there is some need to take money away from education, away from agricultural reform, away from social welfare; there is some need to accept increasing levels of radioactivity in our water and in our air; there is some need to accept government intervention in what used to be open political processes; some need for security clearance; and some need for mail cover to make sure that my mail doesn't indicate that I have become an increasingly serious security risk.

People acquiesce in these things because, somehow or other, they have been persuaded partly that it is necessary and partly that there is not a lot that they can do about it anyway. There is usually some mix. In the process, somebody comes up and says to people, "What we need is a world government." We have had many opinion surveys in many parts of the world, and you can get people to say, "Yes, I am all for world government." You get a 98 percent affirmative response. Then you start putting in the qualifiers: "Would you want a world government that has the following capacity?" It drops to about 80 percent. "Then suppose you could do this?" It drops to about 40 percent. "Then suppose the world government could decide whether or not your armed forces should be abolished?" It drops to 5 percent.

The point is that we are engaged in an arms race of one or another pair of nations at different points in history in each of which case we get reinforcement of existing values; first, of a willingness to accept the idea that the political elites know what they are doing, which has certainly got to go down in history as one of the greatest frauds of all times. The medicine men in primitive societies are functionally equivalent to political elites in today's societies. They don't know what they are doing in the veritable sense that they do not know with any degree of high probability what would be the likely consequences of their political actions. They will never know until we bring the scientific mode to bear. Second, they don't know what they are doing in the moral sense, because what they are doing is creating the environment, creating the set of values, creating the set of expectations that reduces their options at the next iteration.

In the United States during 1977 and 1978, we saw a classic example of a repetitive historical process in which a president comes in dedicated to the idea that the arms race is costly and dangerous. He is going to slow it down, cap it, and then gradually reverse it. And what does this poor character do? He ends up discovering that he has inherited a set of values and beliefs and expectations in his society that make it hard even to get something as measly as SALT II through the United States Senate. In the United States we find the burgeoning of organizations like the Committee on the Present Danger. He finds that shortly after he comes into office, new study groups are put together in the Pentagon and in the Arms Control Agency as well as in all of the think tanks, to once again resurrect that charming idea of, not a war-deterring military doctrine, but a war-winning military doctrine.

We have seen the White House capitulate to the hawkish components in the United States in order to achieve some small, insignificant step on the road to slowing and reversing the arms race. Any social scientist can tell you that if you strengthen the enemy at home in order to get his support, he is going to be stronger the next time around. And that has been the history of efforts since World War II to achieve disarmament. Some other consequences flow. One of the others is that people are persuaded that somehow or other—and this is usually not very well articulated—it is okay to threaten with nuclear weapons and to anticipate using nuclear weapons against foreigners.

Eric Erikson and a number of other psychoanalytic people in the anthropology field have come up with a very important concept which they call "subspeciation." Subspeciation is a very invidious psychological process. The first step is a strong sense of cultural, national, linguistic, or religious identity. In the second step, once we have this identity, "who are we," it is very simple to say "we are different from them," and we now know that the rest of the world is made up of foreigners. Once you have the rest of the world identified as foreigners, they are not only different; they are inferior. You psychologically end up believing that there are certain things that you would never do at home that are quite legitimately done to the enemy abroad, the potential enemy or the real enemy. Now this process goes on, gets reinforced, gets legitimized. Let's say you belong to the functionalist school—and I certainly interpret much of what Robert Muller said as reflecting the functional school toward world peace: all this bridge building, all this marvelous cooperation, and all this looking in global perspectives. As for these physicists and these biologists and these chemists who take a global view of climatology and oceanography, it would take something like three weeks to have these same people working on a top-secret weapons project, the intent of which is to obliterate large fractions of the people in other nations.

Charlie Osgood circulated before the meeting the article from The Progressive magazine about the mentality and the values of the boys who make and refine and man American nuclear weapons. These are nice, clean cut, wholesome American men. And the same thing with these scientists who go to these three or four conferences a year: I know these people; I work with them in a biochemical institute; they have a very global perspective. But I talk to them abut American military doctrine, and all of a sudden what am I hearing? "Well, look what the Soviets are doing." These are supposed to be scientific fellows. They're supposed to be intelligent people. They're supposed to be humane and global. What I'm saying is that these guys are not morally inferior. These are standard human products of a social process that is an integral part of an arms race.

Let me introduce another empirical finding. One of the things we've discovered in our project is that if a randomly selected pair of major powers from over the last 160 years find themselves in a military confrontation, they have only an 11 percent probability of going to war; that is, almost 90 percent of the military confrontations that we've seen among major powers since the Congress of Vienna did not end up in war. If these two major powers also happen to be engaged in an arms race, there is an 80 percent likelihood of their going to war. That's a pretty scary finding. It's the kind of thing policymakers ought to know about. They ought to know, and I guess it's a very sad thing to say, that in international politics, history has been repeating itself with deadly regularity. We have discovered all kinds of cyclical patterns, all kinds of periodicities—the same series of mistakes and blunders over and over and over. It seems to me not only that we have some empirical demonstration that arms races are very dangerous, but I'm suggesting that whether they end up in war or not still doesn't make it a matter of political indifference, because the arms races themselves help to perpetuate the values, help to perpetuate the global perspectives, the parochial perspectives, and perhaps more important than anything else, help to legitimize the distribution of attitudes and the distribution of power in these various societies.

From this it follows that we've got to find a way to break out of this arms race and break out of other arms races, and it's not going to be through consciousness raising. It's going to be through the application of relatively hard evidence and relatively systematic knowledge. You're quite right, Mr. Muller, the social scientists have done a poor job; and as I've suggested, most of the world's physical and biological scientists, when the chips are down, are in the service of their particular parochial, national interests. Take every social scientist that works from a global perspective; I think, looking at Elise Boulding and myself, that you have two counter examples, and I think Laszlo clearly falls in this category. But for every one of us, there are hundreds, maybe thousands, who will drop anything if somebody says, "Hey, for two hundred bucks a day I want you to come down to the Ministry of Defense for three days and write a paper on the evil viciousness of country X's military strategy" or "I want you to prepare a five-man-day memorandum on the wisdom and beauty of our own country's foreign policy, or our foreign aid policy, or our military doctrine." Scientists are as much for sale today as they have ever been. Unhappily, the social scientists are still not getting two or three hundred bucks a day, but the point is that the arms race itself is a major, self-amplifying, self-perpetuating mechanism that prevents us from ever developing and getting legitimacy for a global perspective.

I want to close on the point about the distribution of power. There is no way that we're going to break out of this or other arms races merely by waiting for attitudes to change, when the way in which we allocate our resources, the way in which we allocate political legitimacy, and the way in which we allocate political clout and economic power is all tied up with the arms race. So the moral of the story is that to disarm, we've got to start disarming. When Geoffrey Pearson summarized in capsule form the proposal I made back in the fifties, I think he read me correctly in saying that the only way to disarm is to disarm.

Some people say that that means immediate unilateral reduction of one's own forces. Charlie Osgood and I and a number of others have experimented in some futurology, pre-scientific manner with ways in which super powers might incrementally reduce their military capabilities without necessarily jeopardizing their strategic deterrent, without necessarily even jeopardizing their limited conventional war-fighting capabilities in the gray areas—the Third World and so forth. There is absolutely no question in my mind as a military analyst that the Soviet Union and the United States are under-armed for any kind of credible first-strike posture and are vulgarly over-armed for any kind of strategic deterrent. As Pearson and I were discussing over lunch, the Americans and the Soviets are now in a terrifying process of moving once again through that inexorable cycle in which nuclear-war fighting becomes the strategic core.

All of us can remember the bad old days of John Foster Dulles, who had a primitive, simpleminded view of world politics. But we could have learned one lesson from Dulles and Eisenhower. I remember sitting in this very room back in the early fifties when we were discussing the arms control and disarmament problem. Everybody was really ridiculing the idea of mass retaliation. The one thing that the nuclear weapon and the intercontinental missile gave us was the technological basis for getting a reasonably adequate, short-run deterrent that didn't require endless addition of a qualitative and quantitative sort for our military arsenals. We could have stopped with something like forty or fifty ICBMs each, and could have had a more stable world than we've got today with all of the clever command and control systems, with the increase in accuracy, miniaturization, MARVs, MIRVs, tried and true MX, Poseidon, enhanced radiation warheads, and the whole business. Every one of these things has decreased the physical security of the world, and every one of these things has brought the world closer to war.

I would end, then, by saying that I hope in the next couple of sessions we will not spend a lot of time on consciousness-raising objectives or on pious, long-range, patient scenarios. I would say that the world is on the verge of war, on the basis of my own research to date. I would say that the world has been on the verge of war every day for the last thirty years. Now there are lots of people who say, "Well, boy, look how stable it has been. We've had limited wars and we've killed, at least since the Korean War, usually no more than eighty or ninety thousand people in each of these small wars." But if I can use an unfortunate metaphor, I was once arguing how dangerous the current, strategic picture is down in Washington, and a general said, "Hey, Professor, come on over here. I want you to look out the window. Do you see any bombs falling?" I said, "No, of course not." He said, "Do you see what I mean? The deterrent is working." And I said, "Well you know, that's just about as good an argument as the one I heard about the fellow who fell out of the ninety-fifth story of the Empire State Building: as he passed the fourth floor, he said, 'See, it doesn't hurt at all.' "

The point is, we don't know when the concatenation of events is going to be such that we go. What I am saying is that if we sit by and watch the next phase in technological improvement with its concomitant next phase of re-legitimizing the idea of strategic deterrents—re-legitimizing through, for example, a civil defense program and a mass evacuation program—legitimizing the idea now that nuclear war is not only fightable, but winnable, all we're doing is making the odds even worse.

General Discussion

O. W. Markley: I just want to say that a cheerful demeanor does not necessarily imply optimism. One can be a long-term optimist and a short-term pessimist, and hope that we learn in the meanwhile.

David Singer: You know, I'm reminded of the optimist Herman Kahn who tells us nuclear war won't be so bad and when it's all over we can do a much better job of urban planning. You know, that's optimism too.

Robert Muller: I have been in this organization, the UN, for thirty years. I am known as the chap who has declared that disarmament is completely hopeless. I've said it for 30 years, and I know exactly why it is hopeless. You are not going to get me to make a speech favorable to disarmament, because it is not going to happen. I'm very well known for this. My colleagues from disarmament sessions hate me enough when they make speeches about disarmament and then I make another speech on forgetting about the whole thing because it's hopeless. So I have no hope as to what you can do, because in two weeks from when we meet you will be in exactly the same situation as today. You will be even in a worse situation. That's very clear. And in ten years it will still be like this. Maybe later on the situation will change.

I've been asked to speak about global values. What I wanted to convey to you today is the story of what many people in this house—as a matter of fact, 90 percent of them—have been working on for thirty years. Now you can blow up this planet if you like. That's your affair. But this group of people who have been working in the economic, global, and environmental field will go on whatever you do or don't do, because we conceive that maybe, if we're lucky enough—and if the stupid militaries do not bring about an explosion or an accident, and after the Middle East situation is resolved and other nonsense has stopped—maybe the sky will be clearer. And then when you wake up, you will find a world which in the meantime has been prepared by those people who did everything they could. This is why we will continue, and I will not be discouraged. I know you are in a hopeless situation, and this is why I would not participate in any meeting on disarmament, because I know it is absolutely hopeless. This is very clear.

David Singer: What you said is very important: that people have to be working in different sectors and some of them have to make optimistic assumptions or make no assumptions, just in order to continue working; and God knows, what you're talking about is the Lord's work. But I think you have to couple that with the frequent assertion that we will never get disarmament. You, like Mr. Pearson, help reinforce the worldwide belief that we will never get disarmament. I would say that those of us who give higher priority to relatively short-run political, military, diplomatic, psychological activity are obviously spitting into the wind; the odds are not very good. But let's say that we don't need to make them worse by saying we've got no chance; obviously, this reinforces the fatalism that leads people to say, "What the hell," and it leads people to come to a conference room like this as the most timid, inadequate, short-sighted palliative kind of solutions. I'd like to see people come in from national governments and say, "We've got a mission here and we've got to find solutions."

Fernando Lay: I'd like to stress two points in my reaction to the very enlightening speeches we just heard in this room this afternoon. The first point is that I disagree with one of the previous speakers—I believe it was Mr. Pearson—who took a rather skeptical view of the so-called long-term perspective. Then he invited us to concentrate on the realistic short-term steps. As is well known, the so-called short-term approach has been followed in the disarmament field for many, many years, since the beginning of the sixties, and the results are equally well known. I think that the long-term perspective is a necessity. If it is not a necessity for any other reasons, it is for at least one: because we need some hope. With the long-term perspective, you at least have the hope that someday the world will change. There are also other advantages: for instance, that you give some sense of direction to the common efforts in New York and the world.

The other point that I want to raise is an opposing view to that expressed by at least two speakers here on the role of the individual. I am, as I think everybody in this room is, deeply moved by the emphases on global visions, global values, global brotherhood, global issues, and so forth. And at the same time, I see that the international situation goes in the opposite direction. The use of violence is the rule and not the exception. The physical elimination of political opponents is again the rule and not the exception. Human rights are violated every day on a worldwide scale. The search for effective peace is pursued by the minority and not the majority; and the list might be endless. In two words, the international situation is a very poor one. I don't want to stress again and again this point, because I am sure it is very present in your minds, so I tried in my very small and very tentative paper to stress, just as a beginning of a possible dialogue among us, the role of the individual.

I believe that the real answer to the global arms race and all the negative forces prevailing should be found in the minds of the individuals. We should try to understand why, at the individual level, this happens in this country or other countries throughout the world. I believe that there is an answer. The question of the tools, of the leverage, of the means of changing behavior is another question which may be dealt with, perhaps at another moment. But at this point in time I want to stress this question of the human being: why the man often prefers violence, why he often does not trust the other man, why power politics or the endless search for more money, career advancement, and more success prevails over the search for other positive values which are in the mind of a man.

I wanted only to correct a little bit the main trend prevailing in the room toward globalism, which somehow detracts from the main problem, which to me is the role of the individual: why the majority is so sick, why we are not able to transport from the individual level to the people at the large level the remedies of, say, psychoanalysis. When the behavior of the individual is wrong, for instance, the individual is put in the hospital to get proper care; and if the behavior is not so wrong, we at least give him some pills or some advice. But we are not able to transport these remedies to the global level. This to me is very important, because a requisite for disarmament—and here I don't share the viewpoint that disarmament is not possible—is a community of intentions. At least it is clear to me, as a delegate to the United Nations, a delegate which is now at his fifth General Assembly, that there is no community of intentions now apparent in any room in this building.

William Epstein: I want to put a question to Muller. I too have spent thirty years in the international organization and I agree with most of what he says, and I'm naturally in favor of globalism and all of the various kinds of globalism. But when he says there's no hope for disarmament, it's a waste of time. Well, if we have no hope, then there is no hope. That's a simple proposition. And if there's no hope for disarmament, how are you going to go about ensuring human survival or a chance for it. Faith? Faith alone?

We have many things that can destroy human life on earth or reduce the human condition to a situation where it's not worthwhile: poverty, pollution, population, all the other problems; but the worst and the most dangerous, the most urgent of all of these, is the nuclear bomb. Now if you don't try to control that, then what are you going to spend all your time on? Are you going to wait for globalism? Are you going to reeducate the world? Are you going to cure the problems of poverty and the development gap and everything else? I ask this question because I have respect for your intelligence. How do you justify what you just said: "There's no hope, it's a waste of time. Let's not waste further time talking about it."

Robert Muller: Disarmament, before it can become a reality, will take a change of philosophy. It is not going to happen in the present system of values. I think that, here, we have a new argument for armament, which has been on my mind for a long time; namely, that even if you do not need armaments anymore for war, you need them nowadays for status. I think armaments are much less needed today for a war, which probably will not be waged. Then you have to find another reason, and status has become a very important reason. In other words, if you are a big nation, you have to have arms. And you have to have these arms because then your scientific and technological development is going to be enhanced from it. Now, even suppose that status is going to disappear. Then you're going to have another argument, namely, that you have to be strong to make sure that you can reach the natural resources from the developing countries and teach these people a lesson so that they will not foreclose supplies. What I mean is that I just do not see, realistically, that the time is even ripe when nations will get together and say, "Look, gentlemen, we're going to disarm." It does not mean that you shouldn't try. But if I look at this planet, again from my Copernican view, what do I see? Now they're moving into outer space with killer satellites. The air is occupied with strategic air commands carrying bombs around this world all the time. Going down, on top of the seas you have ships with nuclear weapons. You go down into the seas, you have submarines. Oh, there is one, very brilliant success: the fact that you do not have any installation on the bottom of the sea. You know why: because you don't need them; they're much more effective when you can move them around on submarines, platforms with little propellors.

This is a reality which is produced and born from the fact that you have a world today which is the outgrowth of an historical trend that has brought into power the nation-state. I think Mr. Pearson has said something very fundamental. I've been thinking about this very often. It is that we can thank God that it is the nation-state that has emerged, because at least it is territorial. So it means that we will not have more than about one hundred and seventy. If you had religions, there would be 5,000; if you had languages, 5,000; if multinational corporations, there would be no hope whatsoever. You can create many more of them. But the nation-states at least have this merit of being territorial. They have been born by history, but they are here. What is reassuring is that these nation-states progressively are beginning to stay within their borders. And this is immensely significant when I compare the situation to what happened when I was young, when my own Alsace-Lorraine was taken five times within the lifetime of my grandfather alone. So there is some progress. There is a stabilization in borders.

But I can tell you very frankly that if I were the head of a state, I would not disarm. Given the situation as it is, I couldn't take the risk. And you, Dr. Singer, have been the most effective protagonist of why arms are necessary. There are many arguments I hadn't thought of, but you've really represented this very well. And this is the reality, you see. Now these will change too. In the first place, the big powers are going to discover that their big power is going to disappear very rapidly. Toynbee reminds us that the big powers, when he was young, practically all disappeared. You have today tendencies among the big powers that make you really wonder how long they're going to be big powers. You see new big powers emerging, and you see alliances between the old big powers because they're scared of the new big powers. It's a completely different situation, and out of this you're going to have a history where new things are going to emerge. But if you tell me you are going to bring together, as we did in the disarmament conference, people who would agree to disarm, I would say, "It's not going to work. Not now." If you ask my assessment, I would say, "Before twenty years, not even a chance." But in the meantime, things will change.

Already, you do not need so many military people. You do not, as when I was young, tell people to hate each other to prepare them for the uniform. Today it's a scientific world. You have switchers and you have much less psychological preparation of warfare, because you don't need the young anymore. As a matter of fact, you don't even have any conscription in the United States anymore. There are certain things that represent progress. The multinational corporations are definitely an element of peace. You tell them about war, and they get upset. They're everywhere. They don't want to have their tankers and all their operations disturbed by war. That's another important element which is helping, whereas in my youth the cannon producers were also the same people who were stimulating war. So circumstances are going to change.

The only point I make to you is that having seen what has happened in this organization for so many years is no reason for saying we should give up trying. You should never give up. You should never give up hope. But in view of the fact that you said my approach was an approach which is putting people into fallacy, I can tell you I'm pretty well known for doing exactly the contrary when people speak to me about armaments. This is why I wouldn't move to the disarmament division—for any price. But having been in this field—I was, in Cyprus, political adviser—I know exactly how these people behave when political interests are at stake. But what I believe is that we can facilitate and we can perhaps bring sooner the moment when the human species on this planet is going to emerge from the nonsense. It will emerge from the nonsense, if not in 20 years, it will be in 30, in 40, in 50, or in 100 years.

This is what I thought this conference had as a contribution: it is to show us that we can help in the process. You have in this organization the potential for reducing new sources of conflict. What we are doing in the North-South dialogue is to prevent another possibility of conflict. We are trying at least to reduce the number of new conflicts we will have tomorrow from transnational corporations, from racism, from all the differences between people. If we work on it enough, it there is enough philosophy in this, if there is enough belief in the human species, perhaps we can switch matters around. This is all my point. And this I will not let be diminished by anyone. I will walk out of this room and just continue as before, because even if what I am doing doesn't give a guarantee for the future, at least it's the best I can do. By doing this, every evening I can sleep and rest and say I have done my duty. Beyond that, I cannot change the world. I cannot improve it.

William Epstein: With respect to the arms race, you say the situation is hopeless but not serious. If you wait, things will change and the nations will take care of the situation.

Robert Muller: I did not say you should wait. I just said that if you tell me that next year there's going to be fifty billion dollars less of armament expenditures, I say "OK, let's make a bet." You know the outcome as well as I do.

Ervin Laszlo: If you look at the arms race or the disarmament process as purely an autonomous process, I think we have very pessimistic predictions. If you look at it, however, as an element in an historical process, there are many other elements including the economic, the social, the psychological, valuational elements, and so on, then we can inquire whether some of these elements may not interact with this very, very difficult and otherwise hopeless process. And this is why we want to bring up such unusual and unlikely things as talking about global community values, psychological perspectives, and, in the long term, institutional mechanisms; so I think here is an area that we could really discuss.

George Brown: I have a question, Dr. Singer, in regard to your confidence in the scientific method. Would you advocate that the scientists, who are so willing to prostitute themselves, should have more training in the scientific method?

David Singer: Yes. But that's like asking me when did I stop beating my mother?

George Brown: It was intended.

David Singer: What I'm suggesting is that even the people who are first-rate physical or biological scientists, when they shift their gaze to a social problem, leave all of their scientific-intellectual criteria behind and proceed to behave like any small-town lawyer or taxicab driver. The social scientists are by and large mislabeled, because for every social scientist who uses the scientific method in his or teaching or research, there are scores who essentially say the scientific method is inapplicable to social phenomena. The scientific method is only applicable to physical and biological phenomena. Remember, it was only a century ago that we were told that the scientific method was applicable only to physical phenomena and not to biological phenomena, and I'm still being told by my colleagues that the kind of research I do can't be done. They keep telling me that I can't measure these things, and I am measuring them. They tell me I cannot study history in a systematic way and discover certain recurring patterns. The fact is that my colleagues and I have been doing this. Now you're raising, of course, the subtle and very central question, What is the relationship between their intellectual problem-solving style and the moral and ethical and normative approach?

George Brown: No.

David Singer: You're not raising that?

George Brown: No. That's just part of it. I would say that human behavior is not rational, and that there are aspects of human behavior that have to be taken into consideration. I'm wholeheartedly in support of what you have said, but I think that in the long run we're going to have to deal with the kinds of things that Mr. Lay has brought up.

David Singer: Well, I wouldn't quarrel with it. All I'm suggesting is that the scientific method will permit us to get a better handle on identifying those contexts within which peole of certain personalities operate and, addressing certain problems, behave in what you call an irrational way. One thing that all of us in the behavioral sciences know is that many individuals who are extremely rational and effective individual problem solvers come into a group and acquiesce in a strategy or tactical solution or a decision that would not satisfy the criteria of rationality. That is, they come up with a policy that has a high likelihood of not producing the predicted outcome. But that is something we don't understand the dynamics of. We don't understand why it is that a lot of perfectly rational people who can balance their budget, who can make reasonably intelligent choices about education, marriage, child rearing, home buying, and so forth nevertheless join a committee and end up doing things that are maladaptive. And we've got a couple of the world's best psychologists right at this conference table. I hope we're going to hear from them on this issue.

Bryant Wedge: I just want to comment. In the first place I don't think we're at an impasse. We're just looking at it. It's a temporary semantic impasse, and I think the very question we're going to raise, Dr. Brown, is where it is. Of course human behavior is not rational. Feelings are not rational, and by definition, the nonrational, emotional is what drives the arms race, if you like. It's not a rational process at all. It does not mean it cannot be studied scientifically. And here is where I really wanted to raise questions and go further on about why the scientific study of the nonrational has not prospered better. I think I have heard the answers from Geoffrey Pearson when he said that national status, sovereignty, and national pride are very important, at least from his point of view; from my point of view, extremely nonrational sentiments, which in fact guided the behavior of this institution in permitting the examination of these very questions. You may recall UNESCO's "factors that cause wars" project and how quickly and how sadly that collapsed and how little support it had. It touches right into those items I think Mr. Lay brought to our attention. And I think the reason you two are not quarreling is that Robert Muller is saying that because of these nonrational factors, so long as the membership of the United Nations is what it is—that is, governments, national states—the disarmament process is inconceivable through the present form of negotiations and attempts to cap it. I want to go into that a little more in discussing this tomorrow, but I do think that you shouldn't say that something is not scientifically studyable because it's not rational.

George Brown: No. I'm sorry. I wasn't saying that. I was saying that I don't think at this point that using scientific findings or scientific methodology with political leaders is necessarily the solution. I think that we need to do much more than that.

Bryant Wedge: I've had the pleasure of arguing with Kenneth Boulding for a number of years about his models of rational man, and as a matter of fact seeing him modify them, though not because of my influence. To recognize that these are all nonrational processes, but nevertheless lawful, regular, and therefore studyable, predictable, and alterable is where I think we have come together in our approach to the issue. I just want to say one more thing. With John Stoessinger, I had the pleasure of examining the United Nations Secretariat members over a period of a year and a half, and we saw people who'd been in the Secretariat from one year to twenty-five years, which was the age of the UN at that time. What we found was that secretariat members developed nationalism to the United Nations. What is this? Attachment of a person to a primary group—an extraordinary, powerful, motivating force that was exactly like the nationalism in the most chauvinistic, small-country person threatened by a neighbor. So the United Nations itself displays these rules in its own secretariat function as their territorial defense and their attempt not to let anything happen that would disturb it, showing that the non-rational rules and defensive behavior rules of any organization will be such as to make it very difficult to induce change. We will always have to accept man as belonging to some primary group, and move from these toward transcendant or superordinate types of membership which bridge those groups. That's where a lot of us move toward networking notions. I think you'll recognize what I am talking about: this loyalty of the United Nations person to the United Nations organization, a loyalty that would keep anything from happening that would rock the boat.

Part III
Threat Perception and Psycho-social Factors

9

Psycho-social Dynamics and the Prospects for Mankind

Charles E. Osgood

Pugwash is the name of a little town in Canada where the first meeting of a group of scientists from East and West, mostly nuclear physical scientists, was held. They were deeply concerned about what politicians and the military were doing with their brainchild. This first conference, held in 1957, was stimulated by *The Russell-Einstein Manifesto* (Bertrand and Albert, respectively), issued in 1955 on the tenth anniversary of the dropping of the first nuclear bomb on Hiroshima. This Manifesto is very much worth quoting (in part), and it sets the theme of my contribution to this colloquium:

> We are speaking on this occasion, not as members of this or that nation, continent or creed, but as human beings, members of the species Man, whose continued existence is in doubt . . . . We have to learn to think in a new way . . . to ask ourselves . . . what steps can be taken to prevent a military contest of which the issue must be disastrous to all parties . . . . Here, then, is the problem which we present to you, stark and dreadful and inescapable: Shall we put an end to the human race; or shall mankind renounce war? [And they go on to anticipate some of the psychological factors involved.] People will not face this alternative . . . . They can scarcely bring themselves to grasp that they, individually, . . . are in imminent danger of perishing agonizingly . . . . But what perhaps impedes understanding of the situation more than anything else is that the term "mankind" feels vague and abstract . . . . We appeal, as human beings, to human beings: Remember your humanity, and forget the rest.

In recent years the Pugwash conferences have been expanding to include behavioral and social scientists as well. But have we learned to think in a new way? The answer must be a resounding *no*. The problem, of course, is how to get from here (old ways of thinking) to there (new ways). New ways of thinking in human societies do not just happen spontaneously; they have to be acquired. I will try to show that our old ways of thinking have *causal*, not merely casual, relation to our failure to solve global problems. And what I will propose for this highly interdependent world is *mutual learning processes* for new ways of thinking.

73

NEANDERTHAL THINKING AND HUMAN TALKING

I refer to certain dynamic processes in human thinking as the "Neanderthal mentality" precisely because they are so primitive and so universal in humans. Most of us recognize these processes in others, but remain blissfully unaware of them in ourselves. Yet the only way any of us can escape their constraints is by recognizing their operation on our own thinking as well as on that of others.

Neanderthal Thinking

Perhaps the most primitive dynamic is what I call Pollyannaism—after the blindly optimistic heroine of a novel by Eleanor Porter early in this century. Put bluntly, it is simply easier for humans to mentally process affectively positive perceived things, words, and sentences (pleasant, gratifying) than affectively negative (unpleasant, threatening) ones. I am reminded of a "Frank and Ernest" comic strip, in which Frank says: "Yesterday, for just one moment, all the world news came into focus for me and I got a glimpse of what is really happening. Boy! I hope that never happens again!"

In our own psycholinguistic research at Illinois, we have found, for example, that it takes significantly less time to simply say "and" in conjoining congruent sentences having affectively *positive* adjectives (for example, "Tom is tall [and] strong") than ones having *negative* adjectives ("Tom is short [and] weak"). Also, with the onset of a slide with a *single* word on it starting a timer and the subject simply saying either "positive" or "negative" stopping it (via a voice key on his throat), it was easier for subjects to "simply get the meaning" of the positive members of pairs (never shown in succession, of course) than of the negative members (for example, *joy* easier than *pain*, *reward* easier than *punish*, *above* easier than *below*, and so forth for seventy such pairs). So it seems that the neanderthals within us keep trying to reject the threatening and seek the reassuring. Humans *are* deeply "Pollyannas."

Psycho-logic is a related dynamic—the easier mental processing of congruent as compared with incongruent sentences. I say "related" because incongruence is itself a kind of negativity. Thus, when we compared congruent sentences, which must be conjoined by "and" ("Tom is tall [and] strong" or "Tom is short [and] weak") with incongruent ones, which must be conjoined by "but" ("Tom is tall [but] weak" or "Tom is short [but] strong"), we found that congruent *ands* were much more easily handled than incongruent *buts*.

Psycho-logic phenomena are also very familiar (and critical) in the real world outside the laboratory, of course. If we like Jimmy Carter and he praises some congressman from East Overshoe, then that congressman is likely to rise in our evaluation, but if Castro praises the same congressman, then the poor guy is likely to sink—both shifts being in the direction of cognitive congruence. Psycho-logic runs rampant in international relations, making bogeymen of the opponents in every human conflict: if WE are good, kind, fair, and so forth, then THEY must be equivalently bad, cruel, and unfair; many Americans found it hard to believe that the Russians and the Chinese could have become enemies; two negatives combined by a negative relation—"Must be a communist trick." Thus the Neanderthal within strives to force a complicated world into his own oversimplified mold, grossly distorting it in the process.

Cognitive stereotypy is yet another psycho-logic dynamism. As our Neanderthal's emotional stress increases beyond some optimum level, his stronger (most habitual) tendencies become relatively more so, and his weaker (least habitual) relatively less so; thus a shift toward blind stereotypy and away from creative flexibility. Paradoxically, the greater the anxiety and need for a novel solution to a problem, the less likely the Neanderthal mentality is to discover it.

A recent study by Peter Suedfeld and associates[1] seems peculiarly apropos here. Applying a type of content analysis (designed to index "integrative complexity") to UN speeches by representatives of both Israel and the United Arab Republics, they were able to show that cognitive complexity dipped sharply during periods of conflict, reaching low points in 1948, 1956, 1967, and 1973, precisely preceding the outbreaks of conflict in each of those years. There have also been many studies on group decision making under stress, indicating that "groupthink"[2] causes reduction in perceived alternatives, reality testing, and moral judgment, presumably as a function of intense desire to maintain group solidarity.

Another pair of reinforcement principles, familiar to psychologists working in both animal and human laboratories, concerns the effectiveness of either positive (reward) or negative (punishment) reinforcement in inducing changes in thinking and behaving: first, immediate reinforcement is more effective than remote reinforcement; second, concrete reinforcement is more effective than symbolic reinforcement. For the problems that face mankind today, these tend to be correlated, with the more immediate tending to be the more concrete (money in the hand for a profitable arms contract; wreck of a bus carrying a load of school children) and the more remote tending to be the more symbolic (contributing to UN disarmament and global peace efforts; expressing to members of Congress concern about potential accidents in nuclear power plants).

When you combine Pollyannaism with these reinforcement factors, you get a very depressing interaction: the more that people can avoid thinking about negatives (such as there being no more fuel for cars or a nuclear accident), particularly when they seem remote in time and are highly symbolic in nature, the less likely they are to try to do anything about them until it is too late. Seated in the backyard on a nice spring day, watching the kids at play, and sipping a beer, the Neanderthal within us simply cannot conceive of the trees blackened and the voices of the children stilled, or of there being no more beer.

Human Talking (and Writing)

Some very fundamental changes in the meanings that humans, in high places as well as low, have for the crucial economic, social, and political symbols of our time will be required if mankind is to reach the year 2000 in anything like his present shape. This theme was most fully developed in a 1971 paper of mine for an audience of political scientists.[3]

Under "Conservative Words" I pointed out that the gap between word and thing increases with the remoteness of the things from immediate experience. The words of international politics are typically analogic: "We" and "They"; we "trust" or "defy" each other; there are "slippery slopes" and physical "rows of dominos." The power of words lies in the ways they abstract from reality, sharpening certain features and leveling others; thus "pencils" are to write with, not to kindle fires with, and one can freeze to death for lack of kindling wood with a pocketful of wooden pencils. We are being led by old men using antiquated semantic maps to guide us through the wonderland of the twentieth century.

Under "Radical Sentences" I noted that the power of sentences lies in the fact that they can be used to assert things about their topics ("*Russians* can't be trusted"), that they can "crunch" words together and change their meanings ("He's a *Fifth-amendment* Communist"), and that they *are* potentially radical, lending themselves to concisely vivid expressions (such as "*She* will make someone a nice husband"), thereby stimulating fresh ways of thinking.

Finally, under "Toward a Semantic Revolution," I first cautioned the reader that there must be rules for breaking rules in sentencing (for example, to produce apposite metaphors like "Billboards are *warts* on the face of the countryside" rather than mind-boggling ones like "The summer breeze *shouted* down the mountainside") and I warned the reader to maintain a healthy suspicion of pat phrases like "mutual nuclear deterrence" and "civil defense." I then suggested that the most important ingredient in a semantic revolution is using radical sentences to compensate for conservative words. And I took a few such sentences from my own thinking about relations between nations to illustrate the point: "The usual motive behind the threatening behavior of one nation toward another is fear. There is no real security in military superiority in a nuclear age. Mutual trust is a result of, rather than a prerequisite for, de-escalation of tensions. Nations cannot retain unlimited national sovereignty while at the same time attaining international security."

SUBJECTIVE CAUSES OF
MANKIND'S OBJECTIVE PROBLEMS

Here I will briefly review some of the major objective problems that face mankind—and show how mankind's subjective Neanderthalism serves to exacerbate these problems. I will organize this survey in terms of four categories: science and technology, resources and the environment, national and international social structures, and the pressures of population and rising expectations.

Science and Technology

According to George Wald, in a 1975 article entitled "There Isn't Much Time":

> We live in a highly lethal society . . . . The stockpiles of nuclear weapons in the United States and the Soviet Union [even] several years ago reached the explosive equivalent of ten to fifteen tons of TNT for every man, woman, and child on the planet . . . . The second threat arises from the fact that every nuclear reactor of any type now at work produces as a by-product plutonium 239, probably the most toxic substance known . . . . The third danger . . . is that no one knows how to store the waste products, which will remain dangerous for half a million years.[4]

Add to this, Bernard T. Feld's concern about the competition in *qualitative* technology, expressed at the Pugwash Conference in 1977 at Munich. For example, cruise missiles—light-weight, pilotless, subsonic aircraft—can penetrate defenses by flying at treetop levels, and the neutron bomb, by maximizing human deaths while minimizing property damage, is an open invitation to tactical use. We have, as Feld says, a "mad escalation toward nuclear oblivion."

What happened in the decade between the mid-sixties and the mid-seventies in the thinking of the military-industrial complex was a subtle shift from the goal of disarmament to the concept of arms control—a concept which puts no real ceiling on the arms race and promises very profitable competition and proliferation. In a paper distributed at the same 1977 Pugwash Conference, Jerome Frank showed how the combination of Pollyannaism and the symbolic remoteness of reinforcement contribute to nuclear proliferation:

> National leaders, in general, are optimists—that is, they believe that the course of action which they have determined will succeed . . . . Moreover, the dangers of nuclear proliferation are not real psychologically because they are indefinite and distant in time . . . . A calculation of the positive and negative consequences of promoting or regulating the spread of nuclear capabilities according to these principles unfortunately yields an overwhelming balance in favor of promotion.

According to Richard Barnet, "superiority" in the nuclear arms race is not attainable in any meaningful human sense; yet military advocates of bigger budgets claim that "capabilities, not intentions" are what count.[5] Why? Because the arms race is a "struggle of nerve," they say, not of hardware, and their superiority could be used to extract political concessions—to say nothing of the power and the profit that accrue, respectively, to the military and the industrial sides of the Eisenhower coin. In the face of escalating military budgets (from $54.1 billion in 1966 at the height of the Vietnam War to $92.8 billion in 1977 at a time of so-called détente) accompanying despair over inflation, cutbacks in most domestic programs, and a frightening national debt ($596 billion), how does the military-industrial complex maintain its public support? There is a remarkable coincidence between heavily advertised "scare campaigns" and the pre-voting debates in the House and Senate—an application of immediate and concrete reinforcement for the public (fear of the Russian bogeyman) and for their congressional representatives (fear of losing support in elections).

Surely any objective observer (from some extraterrestrial civilization) would conclude that mankind has gone insane. And it is a collective insanity, shared by whole societies. If individuals were to display similar symptoms (say, a Sam and an Ivan), society would brand them as paranoid and put them away. But when Neanderthal thinking permeates a whole society, it is the deviants that are likely to be called insane. Interestingly, Americans apply this reasoning to the Communists who put their own dissidents into mental institutions, but not to American society.

Resources and the Environment

It is estimated that if we were to stop all use of spray-cans now, we will already [in 1975] have lost about 10 percent of the ozone (layer). . . . [The] workplaces are at least as big a killer [as the automobile]. We register about 22,000 deaths by industrial accident every year, and 2.2 million disabling injuries—but those statistics don't touch the slow killing: the black lung . . . the brown lung . . . the silicosis, asbestosis, and uranium poisoning, and the variety of cancers associated with these conditions . . . . Such statistics are hard to come by, because industry fights tooth and nail to keep them concealed.[6]

The problems of energy and environmental destruction and pollution are intimately related, of course. The national energy plan proposed by President Carter, which he called "the moral equivalent of war," was already a compromise with the energy-producing industries. And in its torturous movement through Congress, it was even more flawed. Something approaching one-fifth of all capital investment in the United States is in energy-producing corporations, and they do heavy lobbying. With much advertising, big gas-guzzling cars have been selling fine. And what proportion of drivers on interstate highways observe the 55 mile per hour speed limit that has saved nearly 30,000 lives since its inception? Another "Frank and Ernest" cartoon has a salesman, standing before a car called "The Blazer," asking our friends this: "First off, do you want to whimper about economy, or do you want to be King of the Road?" Apart from energy per se, there has been rapid depletion of natural resources of all sorts, along with destruction and pollution of the environment. The "have" countries have been operating as if there were an unlimited supply of resources such as aluminum and other metals critical for various high-level technologies, diverse wood products deemed essential for their "way of life," and even sources of basic foods from the land (rice, grains, sugars) and the oceans (fish and crustacea).

National and International Social Structures

David Novick, referring to the have countries such as the United States, says, "We have to swallow a really bitter pill—reducing our standard of living."[7] Americans have done this before, at times of war and during the great depression, but now they must be *induced* to do it in the absence of any enemy or even any immediately obvious catastrophe. What will be required is a complete turnabout in our "way of life," from one designed for conspicuous consumption, stimulated via mass media advertising—so gratifying to the immediate profit motives of people in industry—to one designed to maximize efficient and equitable utilization of the available resources of our planet.

But exactly the reverse process has been developing at a rapidly accelerating pace. Multinational corporations, based mainly in the rich and powerful nations of the West, are expanding out over the globe, gouging from the have-nots to bring even higher standards of living to the haves. And these corporations are making incredible profits from this rather one-sided exchange; some of the largest multinationals are wealthier than many small nations on our shrinking planet. Since the highest level of real political authority is the nation-state, this economic expansion is going on practically without any effective controls.

It would seem obvious that a strong international government is required to monitor and contain this global phenomenon. Yet the Neanderthals within have resisted any movement toward internationalism—such as the ratification of the agreement to turn control of the Panama Canal over to the country which contains it by year 2000. In his 1975 article, George Wald goes so far as to suggest that "our so-called free world is now wholly controlled by such multinational super-entities as General Motors, Exxon, the Chase Manhattan Bank, ITT, Dutch Shell, and British Petroleum. It is no accident that we lack a politics that might change our society."[8]

Pressures of Population and Development

Probably the most important underlying problem of mankind is the pressure of an exponentially increasing population. According to James Echols, given the 1975 rates (total fertility, 4.5; life expectancy, 55 years), the world population will theoretically reach 24 billion by the year 2075.[9] Obviously, our planet's resources would not be able to support such a population. As far as the have nations are concerned, it is clear that the destruction of our ozone layer and our pollution of the environment is in no small part a function of the sheer numbers of people pushing the buttons, being kept warm in the winter and cool in the summer, and tossing their refuse around. And who can blame the have-not countries for wanting a share of this "economic pie"—a kind expression for what is called "development"?

There are many regions of the world where "development" is literally impossible—given the model of have nations, in which "development" is equated with industrial economic prosperity. Richard Lee Clinton claims that neither the capitalist nor the socialist approach to development will be successful as long as industrialization remains a leading strategy.[10] The problems of population and development relate to the struggle of the have-nots to raise their standard of living, particularly since development in this sense has typically been accompanied by lower fertility rates. And in an equitably balanced interdependent world, there would be no necessary correlation between standard of living and level of industrialization for individual countries, any more than there is for individual states of the United States.

On the side of the underdeveloped countries, the grim truth of the matter is that if increasing food supplies are not accompanied by birth control, then population production will outrun food production by the year 2000 at the latest. Of course, procreation is a prime example of immediate and concrete reinforcement—to which, in underdeveloped countries, is added remote symbolic reinforcement of support in one's old age. The relative failure of the government in India to damp the national birthrate contrasts with the relative success in mainland China, where strong community social pressures have been applied. As cruel as it may sound, transmission of food supplies from haves to have-nots may have to be made contingent upon efforts by the latter to damp their population growth.

On the side of the overdeveloped countries, an equally grim fact is that within the past decade or so there has been a sudden increase in demand for beef and pork. Producing meat is a bad nutritional bargain, because it takes about eight pounds of grain to make just one pound of meat. George Borgstrom, cited by Wald, has calculated that world livestock consumes enough feed materials to nourish 15 billion persons. The obvious answer is to shift the dietary habits of affluent peoples in the have countries, which would not only be most intensely resisted by these peoples, but would also be fought tooth and nail by the agriculture and food industries.

THE PSYCHODYNAMICS OF ARMS RACES
AND PEACE RACES

Arms Races

The psychodynamics of "uncalculated" escalation into arms races follow directly from the nature of Neanderthal thinking and talking. Following the dictates of psycho-logic, Mr. Everyman easily turns the WEs into heroes and the THEYs into villains, thereby forcing any conflict in which his WEs are involved into a kind of holy war. Given his Pollyannaish bent, attempting to grasp onto the reassuring and push away the threatening aspects of his world, the Neanderthal mentality leads Mr. Everyman to believe claims that WE are falling behind THEM in military strength and therefore to support demands for more and more billions to guarantee that WE are the strongest nation on earth. Given his tendency toward cognitive stereotypy, paradoxically, the more his anxieties are increased by events—or, more often, by scare stories in the mass media—the more difficult the Neanderthal in him makes it for him to even comprehend any alternatives. And, since Mr. Everyman is less influenced by reinforcements that are remote and symbolic than he is by those that are immediate and concrete, he simply does not have the creative imagination to make immediate and concrete the horrors of nuclear catastrophes.

"Calculated" escalation, described by Herman Kahn as "a competition in resolve" and "a competition in risk-taking,"[11] is a strategy that relies for its success upon the Neanderthal mode of thinking in humans, in high places as well as low. It is designed to push the villainous THEYs beyond their risk ceiling before the heroic WEs reach ours. This strategy has four salient features: first, the steps are unilaterally initiated (we did not negotiate with the North Vietnamese about increasing the tempo of our bombing or moving it closer to Hanoi; we just did it unilaterally). Second, each step propels the opponent into reciprocating if he can, with more aggressive steps of his own (our development of multiple nuclear warheads propels the Soviets into analogous developments). Third, such steps are necessarily graduated in nature—by the unpredictability of technological breakthroughs, by the limitations imposed by logistics, and by the oscillating level of perceived threat. But, fourth, calculated escalation is obviously a *tension-increasing* process, the termination of which is a *military* resolution (victory, defeat, or in our time, even mutual annihilation).

Peace Races

Now, if we change this last feature of calculated escalation and shift it from tension-induction to tension-reduction, we have the essence of a calculated de-escalation strategy in conflict situations. It is one in which nation A devises patterns of small steps, well within its own limits of security, designed to reduce tensions and induce reciprocating steps from nation *B*. If such unilateral initiatives are persistently applied and reciprocation is obtained, then the margin for risk taking is widened and somewhat larger steps can be taken. Both sides, in effect, begin edging down the tension ladder, and both are moving—within what they perceive as reasonable limits of national security—toward a political rather than a military resolution. Needless to say, successful application of such a strategy assumes that both parties to a conflict have strong motives to get out of it.

The focus of my own long-term concern at the inter-nation level has been the rationalization of a strategy alternative whose technical name is "Graduated and Reciprocated Initiatives in Tension-reduction." While doodling at a conference in the early sixties, I discovered that the initials of this mind-boggling phrase spelled GRIT, and although I generally take a dim view of acronyms, this one was not only easy for people to remember, but also suggested the kind of determination and patience required to successfully apply it. One of the aims of GRIT is to reduce and control international tension levels. Another is to create an atmosphere of mutual trust within which negotiations on critical military and political issues can have a better chance of succeeding; in other words, GRIT is not a substitute for the more familiar process of negotiation, but rather a parallel process designed to enable a nation to take the initiative in a situation where a dangerous "balance" of mutual fear exists—and, to the degree successful, GRIT smooths the path of negotiation.

However, being unconventional in international affairs, the GRIT strategy is open to suspicion abroad and resistance at home. Therefore, it is necessary to spell out the ground rules under which this particular "game" should be played, to demonstrate how national security can be maintained during the process, how the likelihood of reciprocation can be maximized, and how the genuineness of initiations and reciprocations can be evaluated. These "rules" are spelled out in detail in my "basic" pocketbook, *An Alternative to War or Surrender* (Osgood, 1962),[12] and were applied to the Vietnam and mainland China situations in another pocketbook, *Perspective in Foreign Policy*.[13]

Rules for Maintaining Security. *Rule 1:* Unilateral initiatives must not reduce one's capacity to inflict unacceptable nuclear retaliation should he be attacked at that level. Nuclear capacity can serve rational foreign policy (a) if it is viewed not only as a deterrent, but also as a security base from which to take limited risks in the direction of reducing tensions; (b) if the retaliatory, second-strike nature of the capacity is made explicit; and (c) if only the minimum capacity required for effective deterrence is maintained and the arms race damped. Needless to say, none of these conditions have been met to date by the two nuclear superpowers. Not only are nuclear weapons ambiguous as to initiation or retaliation, but both strategic and tactical weapons are redundantly deployed and in oversupply as far as capacity for graded response to aggression is concerned. Therefore, at some stage in the GRIT process, graduated and reciprocated reductions in nuclear weapons, along with the men that are assigned to them, should be initiated.

Rule 2: Unilateral initiatives must not cripple one's capacity to meet conventional aggression with appropriately graded conventional response. Conventional forces are the front line of deterrence, and they must be maintained at rough parity in regions of confrontation. But the absolute level at which the balance is maintained is variable. The general rule would be to initiate unilateral moves in the regions of least tension and gradually extend them to what were originally the most tense regions.

Rule 3: Unilateral initiatives must be graduated in risk according to the degree of reciprocation obtained from an opponent. This is the self-regulating characteristic of GRIT that keeps the process within reasonable limits of security. If bona fide reciprocations of appropriate magnitude are obtained, the magnitude and significance of subsequent steps can be increased; if not, then the process continues with a diversity of steps of about the same magnitude of risk. The relative risk thus remains roughly constant throughout the process.

Rule 4: Unilateral initiatives should be diversified in nature, both as to sphere of action and as to geographical locus of application. The reason for diversification is twofold. First, in maintaining security, diversification minimizes weakening one's position in any one sphere (such as in combat troops) or any one geographical locus. Second, in inducing reciprocation, diversification keeps applying the pressure of initiatives having a common tension-reducing intent (and, hopefully, effect), but does not "threaten" the opponent by pushing steadily in the same sphere or locus and thereby limiting his options in reciprocating.

Rules for Inducing Reciprocation. *Rule 5:* Unilateral initiatives must be designed and communicated so as to emphasize a sincere intent to reduce tensions. Escalation and de-escalation strategies cannot be "mixed" in the sense that military men talk about the "optimum mix" of weapon systems. The reason is psychological: reactions to threats (aggressive impulses) are incompatible with reactions to promises (conciliatory impulses); each strategy thus destroys the credibility of the other. It is therefore essential that a complete shift in basic policy be clearly signaled at the beginning. The top leadership of the initiating power must establish the right atmosphere by stating the overall nature of the new policy and by emphasizing its tension-reducing intent. Early initiatives must be clearly perceived as tension reducing by the opponents in conflict situations, must be of such significance that they cannot be easily discounted as "propaganda," and they must be readily verifiable. To avoid "self-sabotage," it must be kept in mind that *all* actions of one's government's with respect to another have the function of communicating intent. Control over de-escalation strategies must be just as tight and pervasive as control over war-waging strategies, if actions implying incompatible intents are not to intrude and disrupt the process.

Rule 6: Unilateral initiatives should be publicly announced at some reasonable interval prior to their execution and identified as part of a deliberate policy of reducing tensions. Prior announcements minimize the potentially unstabilizing effect of unilateral acts, and their identification with total GRIT strategy helps shape the opponent's interpretation of them. However, the GRIT process cannot *begin* with a large, precipitate, and potentially destabilizing unilateral action. It is this characteristic of Senator Mansfield's proposal in May of 1971 (to cut by about half the United States forces permanently stationed in Europe in one fell swoop) that would have been most likely to destabilize NATO/Warsaw Pact relations, to threaten our allies, and possibly encourage Soviet politico-military probes.

Rule 7: Unilateral initiatives should include in their announcement an explicit invitation to reciprocation in some form. The purpose of this "rule" is to increase pressure on an opponent by making it clear that reciprocation of appropriate form and magnitude is essential to the momentum of GRIT, and to bring to bear pressures of world opinion. However, exactly specifying the form or magnitude of reciprocation has several drawbacks: having the tone of a demand rather than an invitation, it carries an implied threat of retaliation if the demand is not met; furthermore, the specific reciprocation requested may be based on faulty perceptions of the other's situation, and this may be the reason for failure to get reciprocation. It is the occurrence of reciprocation in any form, yet having the same tension-reducing intent, that is critical. Again speaking psychologically, the greatest conciliatory impact on an opponent in a conflict situation is produced by his own, voluntary act of reciprocating. Such behavior is incompatible with his Neanderthal beliefs about the unalterable hostility and aggressiveness of the initiators, and once he *has* committed a reciprocating action, all of the cognitive pressure is on modifying these beliefs.

Rules for Demonstrating the Genuineness of Initiatives and Reciprocations.
Rule 8: Unilateral initiatives that have been announced must be executed on schedule regardless of any prior commitments to reciprocate by the opponent. This is the best indication of the firmness and bona fides of one's own intent to reduce tensions. The control over what and how much is committed is the graduated nature of the process; at the point when each initiative is announced, the calculation has been made in terms of prior-reciprocation history that this step can be taken within reasonable limits of security. Failure to execute an announced step, however, would be a clear sign of ambivalence in intent. This is particularly important in the early stages, when announced initiatives are liable to the charge of "propaganda."

Rule 9: Unilateral initiatives should be continued over a considerable period, regardless of the degree or even absence of reciprocation. Like the steady pounding on a nail, pressure toward reciprocating builds up as one announced act follows another announced act of a tension-reducing nature, even though the individual acts may be small in significance. It is this characteristic of GRIT which at once justifies the use of the acronym and which raises the hackles of most military men. But the essence of this strategy is the calculated manipulation of the intent component of the "perceived-threat-equals-capability-times-intent" equation. It is always difficult to read the intentions of an opponent in a conflict situation, and they are usually very complex. In such a situation, GRIT can be applied to consistently encourage conciliatory intents and interpretations at the expense of aggressive ones.

Rule 10: Unilateral initiatives must be as unambiguous and as susceptible to verification as possible. Although actions do speak louder than words, even overt deeds are liable to misinterpretation. Inviting opponent verification via direct, on-the-spot observation or via indirect media observation (such as televising the act in question), along with requested reciprocation in the verification of his actions, is ideal; what little might be lost in the way of secrecy by both sides might be more than made up in a reduced need for secrecy on both sides. However, both the United States and the USSR have long exhibited intense suspicion of each other and placed a heavy emphasis upon secrecy. This poses serious questions for the criteria for unambiguousness of unilateral initiatives and verifiability of reciprocations. However, the strategy of GRIT can be directly applied to this problem. Particularly in the early stages, when the risk potentials are small, observers could be publicly invited to guarantee the verifiability of doing what was announced, and although entirely *without* explicit insistence on reciprocation by the opponent, the implication would be strong indeed. Initiatives whose validities are apparently very high should be designed (for example, initial pullbacks of forces from border confrontations), and they can operate to gradually reduce suspicion and resistance to verification procedures. This should accelerate as the GRIT process continues.

Over the past fifteen years or so there has been considerable experimentation with the GRIT strategy, but mostly in the laboratory. For an excellent interpretive review of this research in relation to the "rules" of GRIT strategy, see a recent paper by Svenn Lindskold.[14] There have been sporadic GRIT-like moves in the real world; for example, the graduated and reciprocated pullback of American and Soviet tanks that had been lined up practically snout-to-snout at the height of the Berlin Crisis. But for the most part in recent history, these have been one-shot affairs, always tentatively made and never reflecting any genuine change in basic strategy.

The one exception to this dictum was "the Kennedy experiment," as documented in a significant paper by Amitai Etzioni.[15] This real-world test of a strategy of calculated de-escalation was conducted in the period from June to November of 1963. The first step was President Kennedy's speech at The American University on June 10, in which he outlined what he called "a strategy of peace," praised the Russians for their accomplishments, noted that "our problems are man-made . . . and can be solved by man," and then announced the first unilateral initiative: the United States was stopping all nuclear tests in the atmosphere, and would not resume them unless another country did. Kennedy's speech was published *in full* in both *Izvestia* and *Pravda*, with a combined circulation of 10 million. On June 15 Premier Khruschev reciprocated with a speech welcoming the U.S. initiative, and he announced that he had ordered the production of strategic bombers to be halted.

The next step was a symbolic reduction in the trade barriers between East and West. On October 9, President Kenneday approved the sale of $250 million worth of wheat to the Soviet Union. Although the United States had proposed a direct America-Russia communication link (the "hot line") in 1962, it was not until June 20, 1963—after the "Kennedy experiment" had begun—that the Soviets agreed to this measure. Conclusion of a test-ban treaty, long stalled, was apparently the main goal of the experiment. Multilateral negotiators began in earnest in July, and on August 5, 1963, the test-ban treaty was signed. The Kennedy experiment slowed down with the deepened involvement in Vietnam, and it came to an abrupt end in Dallas.

Had this real-world experiment in calculated de-escalation been a success? To most of the initiatives taken by either side, the other reciprocated, and the reciprocations were roughly proportional in significance. What about psychological impact? I do not think that anyone who lived through that period will deny that there was a definite warming of American attitudes toward Russians, and the same is reported for Russian attitudes toward Americans. The Russians even coined their own name for the new strategy, "the policy of mutual example."

The novelty of GRIT raises shrieks of incredulity from hawks and clucks of worry even from doves. The question I am most often asked is this: Doesn't any novel approach like this involve too much risk? Anything we do in the nuclear age means taking risks. To escalate conflicts that involve another nuclear power unquestionably carries the greatest risk. Simply doing nothing— remaining frozen in a status quo that is already at much too high a level of force and tension—is certainly not without risk over the long run. GRIT also involves risk. But the risking comes in small packages. Looked at in a broad perspective, the superpower confrontation has many positive elements in it and many motivations on both sides that favor détente. It therefore offers itself as a potential proving ground for a strategy that is novel but yet appropriate to the nuclear age in which we are trying to survive. The assumption behind nuclear deterrence—that we can go spinning forever into eternity, poised for mutual annihilation and kept from it only by fragile bonds of mutual fear—is untenable. The ultimate goal must be to get out from under the nuclear sword of Damocles by eliminating such weapons from the human scene.

ONE WORLD OR NO WORLD

Given our objective and subjective states, what are mankind's prospects? I think that nearly all objective problems could be resolved as we move toward the year 2000, but not by science and technology alone. We must also address the subjective problems and somehow meet the Russell-Einstein challenge by trying to create a massive change in our ways of thinking. But to change ways of thinking (psychological processes) as well as ways of living together (social and political systems) is extraordinarily difficult. We must change ways of thinking *about* the objective problems:

- About the military-industrial misuse of science and technology. We are now hovering in the state of *M*utual *A*ssured *D*estruction (MAD) in the nuclear confrontation of the two superpowers.
- About the economic and social misuse of energy and the environment. Exhaustible coal and oil resources are being rapidly consumed by power plants and the voracious automobile, while inexhaustible sources of energy from the sun, the winds, and the tides have hardly been tapped—in part, because they cannot be turned on and off to maximize profits.
- About the pressures of population and rising expectations. Although being objective conditions, these pressures are man-made and subject to change, albeit not easily.
- About the basic inappropriateness of our national and international social structures—our independent nation-states as the highest political units in a world where they are, in just about all other respects, highly interdependent.

What we must try to do is buy more time—time to allow people in decision-making positions to think rather than simply react habitually to the day-to-day crises. The GRIT strategy I have described is one way of doing this—by calculatedly reducing tensions in areas of high conflict. I might note that GRIT, being by no means limited to inter-nation conflicts, is being applied quite normally and frequently from familial up through all levels of human social systems *except* the highest international level. Time is needed for our humanness—via the use of creative imagination—to allow the more remote goals for mankind to take precedence over the more immediate, and thereby overcome our Neanderthalism.

However, given the primitive nature of Pollyannaism and psycho-logic, I do not think we can buy enough time to have much effect upon public thinking. But in private thinking, particularly of leaders in all fields, we can. Such people should also be better able to break out of the bonds of cognitive stereotypy and use radical sentences to compensate for the conservative words of their languages. They should also be more resistant to the combination of Pollyannaism (denial of the unpleasant) with immediate and concrete reinforcement (for example, power and/or profits), which, as I noted earlier, is a most disturbing and dangerous interaction.

Now let me say something really horrifying: I think one of the most useful things that could happen is a genuine and major nuclear accident, in either military or energy systems, with full television coverage. This would bring the problem into focus; there would be no Pollyannaistic denial possible and there would be immediate and concrete reinforcement for changing thinking; and the deaths of even hundreds of thousands of people might result in decisions which, in the long run, could lead to saving the lives of many millions of humans.[16] In the early 1970s, as I recall, there had been all kinds of complaints from citizens in Chicago about the sloppy and dangerous way the urban transit was being run, but nothing was done until there was a major disaster; then there was a complete overhaul of the system.

A basic issue is "ego-ism" versus "alter-ism" in the conduct of human affairs. Ego-ism is simply the flowering of Darwinian dynamics of evolution (survival—and profit—of the fittest) into an age when one species, humanoid primates, dominates the earth. Yet, most interestingly, it is this species that (not innately, like the ant, but adaptively through learning) has found that ego-ism *can* be satisfied within alter-istic social structures. Quite simply, alter-ism is putting the welfare of others above the welfare of the self, with the realization that, in the long run, one's own welfare is intimately tied to that of others. I think individuals who are profiteering in the proliferation of nuclear capabilities across the planet would realize, if they just took off a few minutes to think quietly about the future, that their own lives and those of their loved ones are just as subject to probability as the lives of all the faceless unknowns; nuclear weapons do not play favorites; fallout falls on yachts as well as suburban homes, and there is no place to hide.

The free enterprise system, which really isn't very "free" anymore (what with collusions of small numbers of giant corporations basically controlling the system), is essentially ego-istic. What we have been moving into rapidly, even if imperceptibly, is what can fairly be called "the new slavery." More than half of all the personal wealth in the United States, for example, is now owned and controlled by only 6 percent of the population; 4.4 percent owns and controls 74 percent of all federal bonds and securities and 78 percent of all state and local bonds. "Of the 23 acknowledged millionaires in the Senate, only three voted against their own pocketbook interests."[17]

Robert Heilbroner highlights the ego-ism versus alter-ism issue by titling an article of his with the question, "What Has Posterity Ever Done for Me?"[18] The rational answer, of course, is "nothing," and why should one (rationally) care about what happens to humans some decades after his own death? Heilbroner goes on to say:

> If there is cause to fear for man's survival it is because the calculus of logic and reason will be applied to problems where they have as little validity, even as little bearing, as the calculus of feeling or sentiment applied to the solutions of a

problem in Euclidean geometry. . . . . It is one thing to appraise matters of life and death by the principles of rational self-interest and quite another *to take responsibility for our choice.* [19]

The most glaring inconsistency of our time is that we humans are already living in a highly interdependent world and yet are trying to run it politically with competing ego-istic national governments rather than with one unified alter-istic international government. A prime example of intolerance of ambiguity in the semantics of international politics is the reification of *nations* as the prime units in international affairs. Since the forests and oceans do not recognize these creations of the human mind, we put up boundary markers, erect walls and fortifications, establish border-crossing restrictions, try to impose language homogeneity within boundaries, define invisible territorial extensions into the seas, and brightly color our maps in different hues so that our children can learn just what is really where—all to reaffirm that the nation is indeed a unitary thing like other things that have names. It then becomes easier to personify nations as actors in a great global game and harder to appreciate either the similarities across boundaries or the differences within. Part of any semantic revolution must be an *increase* in the ambiguity of nation names, by using language that deliberately levels distinctions between nations and sharpens differences within them. This implies gradual dissolution of the nation-state as the prime political unit—which, surely, is heresy!

Given this way of thinking and talking about our world, there is intense resistance, particularly in the have nations, to any moves to shift political power to our existing international government, the United Nations. We have seen this repeatedly in UN-sponsored conferences on problems that are obviously international in scope, such as the still ongoing debate on protection and utilization of the seas on which all mankind depends. The fundamental change that must be made is a division of powers between competing nation-state governments and a unified inter-nation government—a vastly strengthened UN. Such a division of powers would be analogous to that between the powers over local affairs retained by the states of the United States and the powers over interstate (national) affairs allocated to the federal government.

Such a change in planetary governance would have immense implications for developing countries, where there is the basic issue of wholesale versus specialized development. Strong imitative tendencies, to "catch up" with the life-style and well-being of the have countries, has led to a general opting for the "wholesale" model (technological, economic, and military development across the board), the theory being that what has worked in one culture can be exported (with appropriate adaptations) to any other culture. This model also is congruent with the assumption that the autonomous, independent nation-state is the "natural," even the "inevitable," form of human social organization. But if we were to move into one world, politically and otherwise, then the whole conception of development could shift from "wholesale" to "special-ized" (the states of the United States are obviously not self-sufficient, varying from the largely industrial to the largely resource-producing). In this way, the unique contributions of particular developing countries could be maximized.

Given the degree of interdependence that already exists on this planet—not only in the production of nuclear materials (proliferation) and their potential use (fallout knows no national boundaries), but also in the world economy (multinational corporate control over the flow of resources), in the effects upon the environment (pollution of the air and the oceans), and even in communications (computerization and satellites)—we have already reached the point in human history where it *is* functionally one world. But where the essentials of human existence are involved—energy, food, transportation, and, indeed, life itself—control should be in the hands of society as a whole, not individuals. There are more alter-istic forms of economic-political organi-zation than either unbridled Capitalism or unbridled Communism (for exam-ple, more enlightened forms of Socialism), and I think this is the direction mankind must go if we are to survive. But it must be *one world*, under strong international control, or there will be *no world*.

In my science-fiction days I used to speculate that, given the incredibly large numbers of energy-releasing stars in our universe (many with planetary sys-tems) and the essential identity of the chemical constituency of it all, there must have been many intelligent life forms spawned. At some point, many of them must have come to what I would call the nuclear threshold, that point in scientific control over the physical world where the power of the atom is discovered. And the question then must have been this: Had that life form, at that point, achieved a *planetary social organization* that could control the new power and direct it toward social development rather than social destruction?

NOTES

1. Peter Suedfeld, Philip E. Tetlock, and Carmenza Ramirez, "War, Peace and Integrative Complexity," *Journal of Conflict Resolution* 21 (1977): 427–441.

2. Irving L. Janis, "Groupthink," *Yale Magazine*, March 1973.

3. Charles E. Osgood, "Conservative Words and Radical Sentences in the Seman-tics of International Politics," in *Social Psychology and Political Behavior*, ed. G. Abcarian and J. W. Soule (Columbus, Ohio: Merrill, 1971).

4. George Wald, "There Isn't Much Time," *The Progressive*, 1975.

5. Richard Barnet, "Promise of Disarmament," *New York Times Magazine*, Febru-ary 27, 1977.

6. Luther J. Carter, "Radioactive Wastes: Some Urgent Unfinished Business," *Science*, February 18, 1977.

7. David Novick, "Facing Up to a World of Scarcities," *The Futurist*, August 1977.

8. Wald, "There Isn't Much Time."

9. James R. Echols, "Population vs. the Environment: A Crisis of Too Many People," *American Scientist*, March-April 1976.

10. Richard Lee Clinton, "The Never-to-be developed Countries of Latin America," *Bulletin of the Atomic Scientists*, October 1977.

11. Herman Kahn, *On Escalation: Metaphors and Scenarios* (New York: Praeger, 1965).

12. Charles E. Osgood, *An Alternative to War or Surrender* (Urbana, Illinois: University of Illinois Press, 1962).

13. Charles E. Osgood, *Perspective in Foreign Policy* (Palo Alto, California: Pacific Books, 1966).

14. Svenn Lindskold, "Trust Development, the GRIT Proposal, and the Effects of Conciliatory Acts on Conflict and Cooperation," *Psychological Bulletin* 85 (1978): 772-793.

15. Amitai Etzioni, "The Kennedy Experiment," *The Western Political Quarterly* 20 (1967): 361-380.

16. See also Bruce Stewart, "Some Nuclear Explosions Will Be Necessary," *Bulletin of the Atomic Scientists*, October 1977.

17. T. B. Mehling, *Washington Watch*, August 27, 1976.

18. Robert L. Heilbroner, "What Has Posterity Ever Done for Me?" *New York Times Magazine*, January 19, 1975.

19. Ibid.

10

Survival in a Nuclear World—Some Psychological Considerations

Jerome D. Frank

The problem of survival today is as old as the existence of organized societies: How is a society to protect itself against others perceived as threats to its welfare in an anarchic world? The universal, time-honored attempt to solve this problem has been for each group to try to achieve greater military strength, either alone or through alliances, than its actual or potential adversaries. This has always led to war. In the past, one of the adversaries always won; so, for the victor, the solution worked.

For psychological reasons to be considered, national leaders still cling to such a solution, even though the emergence of weapons with possibly unlimited destructive power has made it not only obsolete but potentially disastrous. To avert the catastrophe of a major nuclear exchange will require the best efforts, not only of civilian and military leaders, but also of members of all professions, among them students of human behavior. This chapter touches on a few of the social and psychological factors propelling humankind toward its doom, and offers some suggestions that might help to avert this fate.

With a few striking exceptions, official policies of nations are determined more by considerations of national interest than by preferences of national leaders based on their personal characteristics. In the United States, the nuclear arms race has been promoted by seven presidents who differed markedly as persons. However, since all policy decisions are made in the last analysis by individuals or small groups, certain general psychological principles are pertinent to an understanding of the behavior of leaders.

From this standpoint, the inability of leaders of the United States and the Soviet Union to break out of an increasingly absurd, dangerous, and wasteful nuclear arms race can be partly understood in terms of the image of the enemy, the psychology of deterrence, and the force of habit.

Like all social creatures for whom membership in groups is essential for survival, human members of any one group are predisposed to distrust and feel threatened by members of other groups. When two groups compete for the same goals, this latent distrust escalates into the mutual image of the enemy.

The enemy image is remarkably similar, regardless of who the enemies are. In general, enemy images mirror each other; that is, each side attributes the same virtues to itself and the same vices to the enemy. "We" are trustworthy, peace-loving, honorable, and humanitarian; "they" are treacherous, warlike, and cruel. Of course, the image of the enemy possesses considerably accuracy. Although the behavior of the enemy may be motivated more by fear than aggression, nations who fail to perceive their enemies as warlike and treacherous would not long survive. Regardless of its validity, however, the image of the enemy impedes resolution of conflict because it tends to be self-perpetuating and self-aggravating for several reasons. First, the temptation to break off communications with an enemy is strong, and this impedes access to information that might correct the image. At the most primitive level, one tends to avoid contact with someone he distrusts. Furthermore, since an enemy is untrustworthy, if we let him communicate with us, he might trick us, learn things about us that we do not want him to know, or reveal some good features that might undermine our will to resist. Leaders on each side fear that their people are so naive as to be easily misled by the other's propaganda.

A second self-perpetuating feature of the enemy image arises from the effects of anxiety on perception. The degree of fear of the enemy depends on each nation's perception of the other's ability to harm it and the firmness of its intent to do so. When national interests conflict, each nation seeks to conceal its true strength and to keep its adversary uncertain as to its next moves. Since the unknown is an especially potent source of fear, to the extent that the scope and form of a threat is uncertain, its capacity to arouse anxiety is increased, and efforts to reduce the uncertainty create oversimplification and rigidity of thinking. As the antagonism continues, each adversary sees itself as increasingly righteous and the opponent as increasingly malevolent.

Contributing to this distortion is what has been termed the "strain toward consistency," the tendency to filter and interpret experiences to fit preconceptions. The enemy image tends to filter out information that would not be consistent with it and exaggerate information that reinforces it. Thus the mass media play up incidents of an enemy's treachery or cruelty and ignore examples of humanitarian or honorable behavior. Along the same lines, the same behavior is seen as being in the service of good motives if performed by our side and as being in the service of bad ones if performed by an enemy. For example, although in wartime both sides always commit atrocities, the enemy's atrocities are evidences of his evil nature, whereas ours are portrayed as regrettable necessities.

Faced with an adversary perceived as treacherous and implacably malevolent in a world without effective international peacekeeping institutions, the only recourse is to confront him with superior force, in the hope that this will deter hostile acts through threat of retaliation or enable us to defeat him should deterrence fail.

Since resort to nuclear weapons would be suicidal, nuclear powers are forced to rely on the hope of maintaining deterrence indefinitely. There are strong psychological grounds for believing that such a hope will continue to be vain in the future, as it always has been in the past.

The essence of deterrence is the attempt of one party to control another by threat of punishment should the latter attempt to perform a forbidden act. This is an inherently unstable system. Since it depends on rational calculations of both parties as to the relative benefits and costs of performing or refraining from the act in question, it breaks down when one of the parties calculates, correctly or incorrectly, that the potential benefits of the forbidden action outweigh the probable costs, or when emotional tensions reach such a pitch that leaders throw caution to the winds. The Kaiser displayed this behavior at the onset of World War I, as did the Japanese leaders in ordering the attack on Pearl Harbor. This is the point when, as Bertrand Russell put it, the desire to destroy the enemy becomes greater than the desire to stay alive oneself.

The policy of deterrence increases emotional tension in the leaders of the opposing countries in many ways. It fans an endless arms race, thereby keeping alive mutual fears. A particularly powerful source of these fears is the encouragement of weapons research and development as each side seeks desperately to circumvent the other's defenses while perfecting its own. The faith that an arms race can be "won" technologically is based on the unwarranted extrapolation of conclusions based on experience in one realm to another realm to which they are not applicable. To be sure, science and technology have solved innumnerable problems, including many long considered to be insoluble, such as splitting the atom and breaking the genetic code. But all such problems are posed by nature, not by fellow humans, and in this lies their crucial difference from arms races. That is, although problems of military attack and defense present themselves as technological, their ultimate source lies in the intentions of the adversary. And since, basically, all humans think alike, each solution by one side is promptly counteracted by the other, especially in a world in which technological knowledge is rapidly diffused.

Nevertheless, leaders of technologically advanced nations continue to pursue the will-o'-the-wisp of technological superiority, motivated in part by the fear that a rival might just possibly achieve a breakthrough that would enable it, even for a very brief period, to attack with relative impunity. The more feverish the pace of research and development, the greater the mutual fear.

The emotional tensions of deterrence are aggravated by the fact that its effectiveness depends on each side's ability to convince the other of its determination to carry out its threat. As Walt Rostow wrote many years ago, "Credible deterrence in the nuclear age lies in being prepared to face the consequences if deterrence fails—up to and including all-out nuclear war." Since all-out nuclear war would be an immeasurable disaster for all involved—antagonists as well as mere bystanders—nuclear deterrence puts a premium on bluffing. Former Secretary of State Henry Kissinger wrote before he was in politics: "Deterrence depends above all on psychological criteria. . . . For purposes of deterrence, a bluff taken seriously is more useful than a serious threat interpreted as a bluff." Thus each nuclear power is faced with the emotionally unsettling task of making credible an essentially incredible threat.

These facts are well known to national leaders. Why, then, do leaders cling to the policy of nuclear deterrence? Here the major psychological factor may be force of habit, the inability to change ingrained attitudes rapidly enough to cope with drastically changed situations. An individual's ways of thinking and behaving are established in childhood, and thereafter become the basis of his psychological security by enabling him to predict his own behavior and how others will respond to it. When faced with a brand-new threat, humans inevitably try to deal with it by a familiar way that has succeeded in the past, even though it is no longer appropriate. The very skills which enabled leaders to reach the top in pre-nuclear times "unfit" them to deal with problems of the nuclear age. They have been trained to play the game under old rules and cannot adjust to the new ones that are required; "trained incapacity." The attitudes and behavior of all national leaders today were formed before Hiroshima; hence, they try to deal with nuclear weapons as if they were conventional ones. The more nonnuclear weapons a nation possessed, the stronger and more secure it was; so leaders continue to try to accumulate more nuclear weapons than their potential enemies, even though this increases the insecurity of all.

It is impossible to reduce and eventually eliminate nuclear weapons as long as nations place their ultimate reliance on violence to protect themselves or advance their interests. This reliance, in turn, remains necessary in the absence of international institutions, the decisions of which can be enforced, for resolving disputes peaceably. Citizens within nations only relinquished side-arms as such institutions developed. Analogously, international anarchy must eventually be replaced by an effective world government. In thinking about how to achieve this remote goal, an important psychological consideration is that the authority of all peacekeeping institutions within nations depends on a consensus of those who support them. Jurists have pointed out that, even in dictatorships, no law is enforceable unless over 90 percent of the citizens comply voluntarily.

Similarly, development of international peacekeeping institutions requires the creation of a *sense of community* of all the world's peoples transcending their national allegiances. This will make it possible for each nation to relinquish some aspects of its national sovereignty to international tribunals and peacekeeping forces.

Actually, unlimited national sovereignty has already been seriously eroded, although national leaders seem not to have recognized it yet. On the one hand, even the most powerful nation is no longer able to perform its historic function of protecting the lives, values, and properties of its citizens. It cannot protect them from devastating nuclear attack or from pollution of the air and oceans—or from the economic perturbations caused by the actions of distant nations, as the repercussions of the policies of the OPEC countries have shown. At the same time, nations, especially the smaller, underdeveloped ones, are relying increasingly on the service functions of the United Nations, which contains the germ of world government. The core of its strength lies not in its political arms, the Assembly and the Security Council, but in such agencies as the World Health Organization, the Economic and Social Council, the World Labor Office, and the World Monetary Fund. The allegiance of citizens to their government depends on its perceived ability not only to provide security, but also to enhance the general welfare. The United Nations is beginning to do the latter for many people throughout the world.

In the past, there was no prospect of achieving a sense of community of all the world's people. But now, for the first time, tremendous advances in mass transportation and electronic communication, especially television and the transistor radio, may be bringing it within reach. We have not, for example, even begun to use the potentialities of international communication satellites to increase international understanding.

With potential enemies, these means offer new opportunities for constant communication without the distorting effects of intermediaries (such as the hot line) and for direct surveillance by satellites. Both of these methods yield more accurate and complete information as to the opponents' intentions and capabilities. In itself, this would impose restraints on preparations for hostilities by both sides.

Social psychologists have shown that the most powerful antidote to enmity between groups is cooperation toward a goal that both groups want but that neither can achieve alone. Modern science has created many opportunities for such cooperative activities among nations. We know from the experience of one such activity—the International Geophysical Year, which led to the treaty demilitarizing the Antarctic—that attitudes of cooperation can be fostered and gradually become embodied in institutions. Scientists have devised dozens of such projects that can be activated as soon as the world's leaders are willing. The most hopeful of these may be projects to control environmental pollution, since it increasingly threatens people of all nations and can be achieved only by international cooperation. Nor does cooperation to this end involve any risks to national security. A striking example was the Barcelona Conference on the Mediterranean, attended by representatives of almost all nations bordering the Mediterranean. Israelis and representatives of Arab states cooperated without difficulty in devising programs directed toward their shared goal of checking the pollution of this body of water, which is essential to the welfare of all of them.

The ultimate resolution of the new threats to survival rests with national political and military leaders. Professional disciplines, however, by providing information and suggestions from their particular areas of expertise, can help to guide their decisions. I have tried to indicate some of the potential contributions of social psychology to the understanding and solution of the new threats created by the nuclear age. One may dare to hope that these contributions, in conjunction with those of other relevant disciplines, may yet be enough to tip the balance in favor of survival.

11
Limits to Technology?
Yaap K. Spek

An essential component of any contemporary weapon system is the communication, command, and control function (CCC). Although, in a technical sense, this aspect can be viewed as part of the weapon delivery system, it is a conditio sine qua non, and as such, dealt with separately.

Complete reliance on high-speed telecommunications for the deployment of global strategic forces, and increasingly for tactical nuclear forces as well, provides the nuclear option with unequalled strength *and* vulnerability. Nearly instant target acquisition, high pinpoint accuracy, and fast damage assessment, coupled with greatly automated decision making, constitute the hardware-control elements of what may be termed a "doomsday machine."

Speed is an inherent feature of electronic technology: in a nuclear explosion, or tempest environment, it is enhanced by eventual consequences of the Electromagnetic Pulse (EMP). Among the parameters of a nuclear explosion—the lightflash, the fireball, the ground shock wave, the air pressure shock wave, the thermal shock wave, dust and debris clouds, initial and residual nuclear radiation, specifically the X-ray, gamma and neutron radiation shock wave—the EMP is a phenomenon most feared by designers of communication equipment.

(Communication blackout, degrading the performance of communications and radar systems, is not caused by the EMP. The blackout mechanism is based on the fact that up to three-fourths of the energy yield of a nuclear explosion may be expended in ionizing the atmosphere. The resulting changes in conditions for the propagation and reflection of radio waves can impair communications from minutes to hours at tens to thousands of kilometers from the detonation point. Geometry and intensities of the burst parameters determine the outcome in a particular case.)

The EMP is an invisible, extremely powerful disturbance of somewhat complex origin in an otherwise steady-state electromagnetic field, which propagates in a homogeneous medium spherically from the point of detonation with the speed of light. It has a rise time of less than ten nanoseconds (trillionths of a second), an intensity proportional to the type and yield of the explosion, decreasing, like all radiation phenomena, with the inverse square root of the distance traveled.

Depending on type of warhead, yield, and geographic circumstances of the explosion, the EMP will induce strong currents of up to tens of kiloamperes in any conductor it meets on its way, such as long runs of cable or conduit, overhead power and telegraph lines, support towers, metallic fencing, railroad tracks, and aluminum aircraft bodies.

The EMP will certainly damage or disable antennas, sensitive input stages of receivers, and memories and other parts of electronic instrumentation at considerable distance from the point of detonation. The great range of severe EMP exposure (far beyond the area of noticeable other prompt nuclear weapon effects) implies that civilian and military objects not normally considered targets can be seriously endangered.

Mainly for these reasons, most nuclear forces would not be capable of much more than a spasm exchange. In addition to yields and numbers of warheads, silo hardness, and the range, position, and mobility of delivery vehicles, current nuclear war strategies must therefore take into account survivability of the CCC component of all friendly military forces. Because there are no alternatives to electronic CCC, nuclear radiation and EMP hardening of *all* military electronic equipment has become a major research objective since the early sixties. It has led to C-MOS semiconductor technology, fiber optics, the construction of plasmapanels, bubble memories, and optical computers.

The proper functioning and survivability of communications equipment, particularly in space, depends not only on its ability to withstand the EMP threat—which may never reach 100 percent—but also on its ability to withstand interception, electronic jamming, and high-power laser light. Efforts to ensure secure communications under all circumstances (which include encryption, distributed computing, switched beam techniques, spread spectrum operation, power management, decoying, in general, the fast expanding field of electronic warfare, electronic countermeasures, electronic countercountermeasures) play a primary role in employment doctrines.

However, the fact that the radio spectrum portion of electromagnetic space does not easily allow for partitioning into exclusive domains may already have led to a search for new types of weaponry. Directed energy weapons seem to be gaining prominent research and development status.

Much of the technology involved in producing a particle-beam weapon is directly related to the development of magnetic fusion commercial power. Particle-beam weapons provide a stream of atomic or subatomic size particles such as electrons, protons, and heavier ions. In contrast, laser beam weapons emit electromagnetic radiation energy. Both proton and electron beams are suitable for use within the atmosphere, because they tend to stay in a channel formed by the beam itself. In space, such beams would rapidly diverge because of repulsive forces between the particles. By neutralizing accelerated ions, however, a beam could well continue its course outside the atmosphere. There is sufficient evidence to suggest that, given the availability of compact, survivable power modules, the applications of space-based lasers for blinding communication and surveillance satellites, or as a defense against ballistic missiles, is a practical feasibility.

However, the status and anticipated role of beam weapons for destructive purposes are far less clear and are scientifically controversial at the present time. Should extensive research lead to an acceptable design—which has to include suitable target acquisition and guidance-precision capability—the following advantages can be enumerated:

- Essentially zero time of flight; therefore, instantaneous target destruction
- All-weather capability
- Extremely fast response time (for example, reduced sensitivity to high-g maneuvering by an evading target)
- No self-induced thermal and radiation blackout
- Minimal release of nuclear radiation
- Low commitment altitudes and ranges
- Testing not restricted by nuclear test-ban

The ability to concentrate beams of energy moving at the velocity of light, so narrow that they overwhelmingly exceed nuclear bomb energy-density-delivery capability, should be recognized as a weapons achievement with implications every bit as shattering as the development of monstrous but uncontrolled energy releases of nuclear bombs themselves. Placing sufficient numbers of laser and beam weapons in space could cause profound changes in the mutual-assured-destruction philosophy upon which deterrence rests. It raises the distinct possibility that the rapid delivery of nuclear explosives can be prevented by a weapon system that is itself not capable of mass destruction.

Such a system clearly would give the nation that possesses it options in strategic posture and activity that are now denied everyone, including returning to those in charge the time to permit adequate decision making, which was taken away by the unholy synergism of nuclear weaponry and ballistic missiles.

Whatever the state of the art may be at present, it is hard to deny that both the electromagnetic domain and outer space, the latter providing the optimal conditions for use of the first, are rapidly evolving into major battle areas. Should such a weapon system come about and a workable doctrine for its use be adopted, it is by no means obvious that (as was suggested in a recent television program) "the ultimate result will be peace."

Conversely, scientific endeavor may have reached a limit beyond which no further military advantages can be obtained. If this appears to be true—if unwarranted expectations keep fueling an effort that in due time may be regarded as a hoax—the consequences will evolve far beyond this stage, it being merely a dangerous moment in the history of the earth. It could, with other emerging factors of global importance, hasten the birth of humankind or of World War III.

At the 1978 Congress of the International Federation of Astronautics, Edward R. Finch, chairman of the aerospace law committee, international law section of the American Bar Association, made some interesting remarks regarding outer space, global interdependence, and the geostationary orbit:

Under the initial remarkable international legal regime of peaceful beginnings, namely the 1967 Outer Space Treaty, several treaties and agreements more specific in scope have since been negotiated; i.e., the Agreement on the Rescue of Astronauts, the Return of Astronauts and the Return of Objects Launched into Outer Space; the Convention on Registration of Objects Launched into Outer Space; and the present efforts dealing with Exploitation of the Moon's Surface.

The most difficult issue—determining precisely what constitutes acceptable military use of space—is the variety of later bilateral agreements that do not have as guiding terms of reference the positive uses of space reflected in the Outer Space Treaty; for example the 1972 ABM Treaty Limiting the Use and Capabilities of Antiballistic Missiles; the Interim SALT Agreement of 1972 limiting the use of certain strategic weapons; the 1973 Limited Nuclear Test Ban Treaty.

Is World War III coming? No. What stops it? Outer space. Does the United Nations make a real contribution to world peace? Yes. Is linguistic semantics and understanding a problem? Yes. Fear of a global World War III must be tempered in the global interdependence context, by a realization that no World War III on a global scale can begin (even on a small tactical nuclear level, escalating to a world holocaust) until the aggressor *first* conquers outer space.

The public is not aware of the necessity of keeping outer space non-aggressive, but it is for this reason that President Carter and Chairman Kosygin of the USSR very recently have agreed to open outer space killer-satellite-ban talks. The public is really not fully aware of the importance of outer space. It keeps open international communications, opens communications between smaller nations, and opens environmental protection for the benefit of the whole world. It helps weather and population control, navigation, and even will produce pollution-free energy from outer space for earth from the sun.

We now have seven nations with nuclear capabilities to start a World War III. In a few years we will have approximately nine nations with world holocaust capabilities. Can we turn these nine nations to the peaceful outer space high frontier? No. Not unless we give them international faith, that they have achieved outer space national security, and do not need to pursue the goals of nuclear war further. Perhaps that can happen.

Science and technology which have evolved because of world fears about outer space (and the resultant expansion of nuclear missiles) is the same technology which can be turned to the greater benefit of all nations and peoples of the world via outer space.

The U.S. and the USSR space shuttles will soon help toward pollution-free energy for earth from the sun, and numerous other benefits for people on earth. International Space Law has kept pace with the outer space new frontier. Let's get a new Lunar Treaty from the UN soon. The key to world peace is outer space. Let's encourage all aspects of global interdependence and encourage the international faith to accomplish it. Keep the outer space keys, and the freely open door of outer space will keep the door of World War III firmly closed.[1]

As to the peaceful uses of outer space, recent technological developments have been such that it is entirely correct to speak of a fast-approaching maturity. A long list of anchor opportunities and realistic long-term projects is well within reach.

Space industrialization can be defined as a new technology in which the special environmental properties of outer space are used for the social and economic benefit of the people on earth. These special properties include zero-gravity, hard vacuum, low vibration, wide-angle view, and a complete isolation from the earth's biosphere.

During the next few decades, space technology (developed for purely scientific reasons, for political and prestige reasons, or to serve specific military needs) can be adapted, extended, and expanded to use the new environment and nearly limitless resources of outer space for the benefit of humanity in an economically profitable manner.

Space industrialization will then grow from a handful of commercially operated communications satellites into a highly diversified and expanding sector of the human socioeconomic system. In the first few decades, however, it will necessarily depend for its very existence on the conventional segments of the socioeconomic system to provide the technology, the original investment capital, and the markets for its goods and services. Thus it is essential to explore the nature and shape of the socioeconomic system as it may evolve in the next few decades before one can realistically examine just what may constitute space industrialization, and how, why, and when portions of the new space industries may arise.

If the limits-to-growth hypothesis should prove to be correct, then perhaps space industrialization could provide some of the very basic needs of the industrialized societies of the world. In all probability, developing nations would soon become prime beneficiaries of space industrialization. Opportunities for space industrialization, currently under serious consideration in the United States, Western Europe, Japan, and with little delay, undoubtedly, in the USSR, China, and India, fall in four general categories.

1. Services, data-acquisition, and information transmission
2. Products, organic and inorganic
3. Energy, conservation, new sources
4. Human activities, space careers, frontier for humankind

In a very real sense, the services of space industrialization are already a reality. For several years, space platforms have been providing valuable communication, navigation, observation, and weather services for people worldwide.

The utilization of satellite technology in arbitrary locations is based on simple economics. The cost of the hardware necessary to handle a satellite voice circuit has been declining by a factor of 100 every twelve years. Moreover, large-scale antenna farms launched by the space shuttle may soon bring about further important cost reductions. Hardware investment costs as low as $14 per circuit-year—down from $20,000 in 1966 and $200 today—seem entirely within the realm of possibility. With costs at this level, numerous new applications of advanced communications become possible.

Evolutionary trends in electronic technology are particularly noteworthy. In 1946, the world's most impressive electronic device, the ENIAC computer, reached operational status. It contained 16,000 electronic switches and was roughly the size of a 5-room house. In 1977 several companies began marketing microcomputers, in the form of solid-state chips with about 4 times the complexity of the entire ENIAC, yet measuring only 5 millimeters on a side. The costs of solid-state electronics have been dropping by a factor of 10 every four and a half years.

By developing the capability to build extremely large multi-beam antennas in space and eventually adding the presence of man to operate, service, and (perhaps more importantly) update the system to incorporate ever-expanding technology, one can foresee systems in the 1980s and 1990s that can broadcast preprocessed information directly to the user. A multi-beam antenna uses a sophisticated feed mechanism to send out several dozen high-intensity beams from a single antenna; each beam covers a different spot on the ground and each utilizes the full surface of the antenna.

With multi-beam technology, pocket telephones, direct broadcast television, electronic tele-conferencing and tele-commuting, and dozens of other developments, all resorting under the concept of telematics, will soon become practical and cost effective. In addition, these multi-beam antennas will allow extensive frequency reuse, thus conserving precious space in our increasingly crowded frequency spectrum. Thus, we see that the trend of the future is to put complexity into space rather than on the ground. This will allow the corresponding ground user sets to be small, simple, inexpensive, and therefore widely proliferated.

Steps leading to large-scale space-processing operations would start with an upgraded space-shuttle orbiter, allowing it to stay on orbit for an extended period of time. Early operations necessary to prove out the processing concepts should result in some marketable products and materials. Subsequent stages consist of small, shuttle-tended free-flyers and a special space-processing section of a manned space base that permits it to make large quantities of high-value products for earth markets. Recent studies indicate that pharmaceuticals, thousands of tons of crystals, glasses, and metal items will probably be processed in space by the turn of the century.

Such large-scale operations will require major dedicated factories that utilize hundreds of kilowatts of electrical power. Space industrialization offers many methods for conserving and augmenting energy supplies. Electronic tele-commuting and tele-conferencing are two examples that could help curb fuel consumption. In addition, energy could be saved by more accurate weather forecasting, and better snow peak measurements would permit more realistic water impounding to increase the production of hydroelectric power.

Large, space-manufactured DC rectifiers would reduce the use of fuel-inefficient, peak-load turbine power plants. Higher-temperature turbine blades, made in space, would also help us conserve our energy supplies. Even a 10 percent increase in operating temperatures would result in annual savings of millions of tons of coal and millions of gallons of aviation gasoline.

The energy that can be intercepted in space exceeds the energy that can be intercepted by a similar facility located on the ground by about one order of magnitude. The energy provided by a solar power satellite (SPS) would be available 99 percent of the time—thus alleviating the storage problems associated with ground-based energy collection systems. For its size, an SPS can be remarkably lightweight, because of the virtual lack of gravitational forces in space and because of a seldom mentioned space-environmental property: no winds. A solar panel covering some 80 square kilometers would generate 5 gigawatts of useful electrical power and weigh only 36 tons. Technology development has now reached the feasibility phase: the next logical step would be to proceed with a demonstration which will help to find out whether the option of obtaining economical, continuous, and environmentally safe power from space can be realized.

Other energy-producing opportunities in space include the Lunetta, which reflects localities on the dark side of the earth, and the Soletta, which reflects substantial amounts of solar energy, typically providing one solar constant over limited regions of the earth, both day and night. The exploitation of new energy sources can also be aided through the manufacture of special deuterium-infused glass spheres for use in laser fusion reactors and by conducting fusion research in orbit.

Human activities in space have excited man's imagination throughout the space program, and they still make the headlines far more frequently than the many other facets of space. The human spirit needs the promise of a better future and the challenge of distant worlds. This era of the "high frontier" marks the first time humankind has ever had a frontier that is only 300 kilometers away from every person on earth. It is to be expected that a flourishing space industrialization program will do much to turn the dreams of colonization into hard reality: thus, in addition to providing real benefits to millions of people living and working on earth, space industrialization will give rise to numerous new earth-based specialties and space careers.

So much for the projections of the space-engineering community. In view of the foregoing comparison between military and peaceful uses of outer space, our latest "common heritage," the question arises whether adequate international measures exist to prevent a disastrous accumulation of conflicts and dangers. A precedent for the regulation of high-level science and technology, where large-scale implications of close coincidence of use and abuse cannot be tolerated, was set with the advent of atomic energy. In 1946, John von Neumann testified before the U.S. Senate Special Committee on Atomic Energy:

It is now that physical science has become "important" in the painful and dangerous sense which causes the State to intervene. It is only now that science as such and for its own sake has to be regulated, that science has outgrown the age of independence from society. . . . From the scientist's viewpoint, this evolution is probably not a desirable one—but nobody can change it, and we must admit that it is taking place.

Since that time, a new case—namely recombinant DNA—finds itself in the same position. The conquest of space may soon join these two cases, which have the following common aspects:

1. Scientific experiments and resultant technology have the potential for enormous benefit and catastrophic disaster.
2. Painstaking care and stringent regulation can drastically reduce the probability that a catastrophic disaster will occur. These cases therefore have the capability of low-probability, high-consequence accidents.
3. Scientists and technologists create products or effects that do not exist in nature, and the protection of public health and safety requires techniques to contain these products or effects in such a manner that they cannot enter the general environment.
4. The health, safety, and security of the public rest ultimately upon faith in the omniscience and infallibility of the human beings who design and implement the scientific and technological endeavors and the safeguard systems within which these endeavors are conducted.
5. All three cases raise substantial ethical, moral, and political issues.

Whereas the DNA controversy draws currently wide public attention, the nuclear issue, after a short-lived public involvement, was smothered by a combination of security-imposed secrecy and a perception of impenetrable technical complexity, both of which were skillfully nurtured by the atomic energy establishment in order to permit decisions to be made by a small in-group rather than through the usual political processes. To this, Harold P. Green, professor of law at George Washington University, adds:

The present morass in which nuclear power technology finds itself is a direct heritage of this calculated paternalism which was finally shattered in the late 1960s with the emergence of the environmental movement. Given today's extremely rapid pace of scientific advance and the escalating destructive (in both a physical and ethical sense) potential of technology, it is imperative that the need for societal controls be fully debated in the political process in the very early stages of scientific and technological development.[2]

Outer space may go the way of atomic energy: obsessed with the concern that restrictions may impede conventional national security considerations, military and commercial super-planners within superpower blocs press for super-projects, the evaluation of which escapes public scrutiny.

Something is seriously wrong. What started as a liberator of the human spirit and held the promise of "happiness and plenty" for all has resulted in inequity, exploitation, alienation, and apathy. Far from being an instrument of human salvation, modern science has gone on a course that threatens survival itself. . . .

Technological optimists arguing that the social pathologies generated by modern high technology can be overcome by more such technology are players in the theater of the absurd.[3]

This statement, taken from an "Indictment" issued by the World Order Models Project in September 1978 at an NGO forum on the 1979 UN Conference on Science and Technology for Development, may sound undeservedly hard, but it does provide an impulse necessary to awaken us from the technological trance. If a careful review could be made of plans still on the drawing board, the overall dangers would outnumber the promises now advocated by a small group whose vested interests are the sole criterion for an eventual go-ahead.

The future well-being of life on our planet has become so delicately dependent on this type of economical-political decision that wide public attention and participation regarding options ranging from organizing scarcity to the further creation of wealth cannot remain unconsidered. In this respect, there is an utmost urgency to overcome the concept of national security, singularly defined in terms of military strength. Since it is now abundantly clear that war no longer can be an instrument for settling disputes, pursuit of suicidal capabilities, mainly devised by the Western scientific community, needs correction toward more constructive undertakings. Let us abandon the fear-driven race to stay ahead of surprise technology, in favor of a positive search for our collective future.

In his book *The Twenty-Ninth Day*, Lester Brown develops the following point of view:

As the deteriorating relationship of man to nature is put into perspective, and as the necessity of accommodation becomes more obvious, governments will inevitably have to redefine the traditional concept of national security. The concern for the security of a nation is undoubtedly as old as the nation-state itself, although only since World War II has it acquired an overwhelmingly military character. Yet concern about military threats from other nations has become so dominant in the deliberations about national security that other threats are being ignored. The deterioration of biological systems, the progressive depletion of fossil fuel resources, and the economic stresses due to resource scarcities all represent threats that derive less from the relationship of nation to nation than from the relationship of man to nature.

Perhaps the best contemporary definition of national security is one by Franklin P. Huddle, director of the massive U.S. Congressional study *Science, Technology and American Diplomacy*. In "Science," he writes: "National security requires a stable economy with assured supplies of materials for industry. In this sense, frugality and conservation of materials are essential to our national security. Security means more than safety from hostile attack; it includes the preservation of a system of civilization."

Dr. Huddle goes on to say that each country should design a way of life that is acceptable to its people and compatible with the needs and choices of the rest of the world.

Increasingly, national security must be tied to the condition of the world's economies and political systems. The stability of these systems is in turn dependent on assured energy supplies and on the stability of the earth's biological systems. National defense systems are useless against these new challenges.

The new threats to national security are extraordinarily complex. Ecologists understand that the deteriorating relationship between four billion humans and the earth's biological systems cannot continue. But few political leaders have yet to grasp the social significance of this unsustainable situation.

It is not that the least able are stumbling, but that the finest minds are missing the mark so widely.

We now confront the prospect that the complexities of the modern world might exceed our analytical capabilities. We must also ask whether existing political institutions can effectively manage deepening interdependencies. Perhaps more important, are we capable of creating and managing the political institutions we need?[4]

Let us hope that the United Nations, with its formidable administrative resources and a considerable accumulation of wisdom concerning global issues, will be allowed to live up to this task.

NOTES

1. Hon. Edward R. Finch, "Outer Space, Global Interdependence, and the Geostationary Orbit" (XXVIII Congress of the International Astronautical Federation, Dubrovnik, Yugoslavia, September 25–October 1, 1978).

2. Harold P. Green, "The recombinant DNA controversy, a model of public influence," *The Bulletin of the Atomic Scientists*, November 1978, pp. 12–16.

3. "The Perversion of Science and Technology, An Indictment," (paper issued at the 14th meeting of the World Order Models Project, Poona, India, July 2–July 10, 1978).

4. Lester R. Brown, *The 29th Day: Accommodating Human Needs and Numbers to the Earth's Resources* (New York: W. W. Norton & Co., 1978) pp. 293–4.

REFERENCES

Conference on Space Commerce: New Options for Economic Growth, November 15, 16, 1978, New York City. Sponsored by New York University and the American Institute of Astronautics and Aeronautics. Proceedings to be published by AIAA, Office of Public Information, Dr. Jerry Grey, 1290 Avenue of the Americas, New York, N.Y. 10019.

Garwin, R. L. "Charged-particle Beam Weapons?" *The Bulletin of the Atomic Scientists*, October 1978, pp. 24–27.

Glasstone, S. and Dolan, P. J. *The Effects of Nuclear Weapons*. 3rd ed. Washington, D.C.: U.S. Government Printing Office, 1977.

IEEE Transactions on Antennas and Propagation, Vol. AP-26, no. 1, *Special Joint Issue on the Nuclear Electromagnetic Pulse* (together with IEEE Transactions on Electromagnetic Compatibility). New York: IEEE, 1978.

Ricketts, L. W. *Fundamentals of Nuclear Hardening of Electronic Equipment*. New York: Wiley Interscience, 1972.

Ricketts, L. W., Bridges, J. E. and Miletta, J. *EMP Radiation and Protective Techniques*. New York: Wiley, 1976. Page 434 shows a table with expected radiation levels for 1980.

Robinson, Clarence A., Jr. "U.S. beam weapon developments." *Aviation Week and Space Technology*, issues of October 2, 9, and 16, 1978.

Space Industrialization. Downey, Calif.: Rockwell International, Space Division, Report SD-78-AP-0055-1-4.

Space Industrialization Study. Final Report. Huntsville, Ala.: Science Applications Inc.

"U.S. moving toward vast revision of its strategy on nuclear warfare." *New York Times*, November 30, 1978, p. A1.

12

Reducing Hurt Feelings and Fear as a Prerequisite for Arms Reduction

Bryant Wedge

On October 15, 1978, the United States Congress authorized the creation of a commission on proposals for a United States Academy for Peace and Conflict Resolution; on November 1, President Carter signed it into law. While this action has scarcely been noticed (the bill appeared as an amendment to the Elementary and Secondary Education Act and was not front-page news), it represents a landmark turning point—the first time in history that a world power has taken concrete steps to establish and institutionalize an organization within a national government to pursue and monitor a peace-seeking and peacemaking policy. I believe this is the first step on the long journey to reversing the war cycle of the last 6,000 years of human history and of reducing the burden of arms on the resources of our globe and the conscience of humankind.

It is now possible to outline, in the rough, a series of concrete and attainable steps to build and set in operation the institutions and mechanisms to reduce the hurt feelings and fears that are the driving force behind wars and preparations for war, which sustain the obscene and costly anachronisms of technologized, industrialized, and organized machinery for mass killing of human beings and mass destruction of human environments, habitations, and products of the spirit. This can be said with considerable confidence, since the action of the Congress certainly represents a striking shift in perception of what is possible, practical, and necessary in the contemporary world.

Actually, as with most shared perceptual shifts, there has been a lengthy preparation and a cumulative amassing of insight and evidence that the war system and the seeking of group security through military strength is obsolete *and* that nonthreatening means of enhancing the security of nations and the values of their cultures—that is, a peace system—is practically conceivable. Here, only two items of this long process will be touched upon: the growing appreciation of the role of hurt feelings and fear in the causation of armaments and war; and the recent and rapid emergence of the social inventions of systematic peacemaking mechanisms.

Let us begin by observing that it is still true that national governments are the dominant social institutions of the last four or five hundred years of the human enterprise, and that these governments still hold a relative monopoly on the "legitimate" exercise of force as an instrument in sustaining both internal order and external "security." And it is still relatively true that governments behave in terms of power theories, whether those of the power balances of traditional diplomacy or of the highly evolved sciences of strategic balance theory and analysis that have occupied so many of the world's most technically sophisticated minds over the last three decades.

What has changed quite swiftly since the founding of the United Nations is our understanding of the forces that drive the behavior of states. While classic political theory considered that national state behavior obeyed axioms of power maximization in more or less rational or "economic man" patterns, there has been a cumulative growth of understanding of nonrational forces determining state behavior; nonrational, but nevertheless humanly understandable, lawful, and regular patterns in the behavior of human organizations. Among these are hurt feelings and fears of the other that feed into and interact in conflict cycles.

Knowledge of these factors has emerged from a dozen fields of study (including, but not confined to, anthropology, economic behavior, historiography, international law, international relations, political science, social psychiatry and psychology, sociology, and philosophy of science) involving tens of thousands of compilations of literally millions of observations.

I may be forgiven for starting by relating a personal experience in disarming angry and frightened men. When I was teaching a class at the University of Chicago in 1952, we heard gunshots in the hallway. As my class and I looked on, a bleeding man in a white uniform staggered from an examining room followed by a shabbily dressed gun-waving youth. I thought I should intervene, but to my amazement, my legs refused to walk. I was left with no alternative but to shout down the hall, "What do you want?" The gunman replied, "I want treatment for my pain."

As a young psychiatrist, what could I say but, "Tell me about it." The gunman came to me, complained that he had been kept waiting although he hurt (perhaps he was acting for thousands of other hurting patients confronted with the medical system) and that he felt he was discriminated against. I told him that his gun made me nervous and that I couldn't help him with it pointed at me. He looked very relieved as he put it in his pocket. And we discussed his trouble, until the police came and took him away.

Shortly after that, I was drafted into the military medical system and went to work in a large army hospital that cared for military prisoners among others. There I was able to put the lessons of my cowardice and nonworking legs to work when, from time to time, a prisoner-patient would "go berserk"; in fact, the provost marshal, the police chief of the hospital, called me with regularity after my odd talent was discovered and when a patient became armed and dangerous. This was repeated ten times over the next two years, and the scenario was remarkably consistent.

A prisoner-patient, most often an undereducated and not very articulate enlistee who had fallen into some quarrel with superiors, would feel himself deprived of some deserved privilege. When his complaints were not heard, he would feel hurt and unjustly treated; soon he would acquire a weapon—a chair leg, screwdriver, or shard of glass, and once a pail and access to boiling water—and at slight provocation he would attack his tormentor, the with-holder of redress. Immediately, force would be brought to bear, and he would be surrounded by police, and even firemen with hoses. He would become frightened, and would flail at anyone who tried to approach. When I appeared on the scene, I would ask the official forces to withdraw some distance, and would inoffensively sit on the floor within easy earshot and ask the same question, "What do you want?" In each instance, the angry frightened man would begin to detail his complaints, and I would soon have an opportunity to ask him to stop scaring me and others with his weapons. In each case, the weapons were given to me and I was allowed to take the person to the officer in charge, sometimes even with his accepting wrist restraints. Of course, they believed me when I said I would negotiate a hearing but could not promise an outcome. And, of course, I always did. They were invariably relieved not to have to carry on their fight, and they said so; they said they had been frightened.

It may sound terribly simple to suggest that quite similar dynamic cycles characterize the behavior of nations, but a vast amount of research has shown that groups and nations in conflict with others are motivated by a shared perception of being unjustly treated, and that anger arises from these shared hurt feelings, however rationalized. Moreover, the adversary is regularly seen as ill-intentioned and armed to some degree. What is to be done but to seek the means of redress and of self-defense? Then, as the conflict cycle is established, the element of fear enters in and the adversary is often supposed to be concealing capabilities and harboring aggressive intentions, thus requiring the maintenance of strength and vigilance in self-defense. Whole vocabularies of threat description are developed, often with some kernel of truth and a very large element of fearful fantasy. Identical processes have been shown to occur in experimental groups of eleven-year-old boys, corporate officers, and gov-ernment officials; they have been demonstrated in public polling of adversary peoples and depth interviews of leaders; they have been validated by analysis of the public speeches of chiefs of state. And, gradually, this knowledge has filtered through into the understanding of elites, leaders, and the publics of many nations; indeed, the public sometimes leads the leadership in appreciating the role that anger arising from hurt feelings and fears of the other may play in magnifying threat and justifying the burdens of arms and military expenditures. One is reminded of President Eisenhower's farewell address in which he predicted that "only an alert and knowledgeable citizenry can compel the proper meshing of the huge industrial and military machinery of defense with our peaceful methods and goals so that security and liberty may prosper together."

Given this apparently universal propensity of men, groups, and nations to react with anger to hurt feelings and to magnify threats from fear, it is not at all surprising or mysterious that they arm to meet real and magnified threats and that arms races continue in the face of all rationality. The problem is, quite apparently, escalated when arms reduction and disarmament are proposed; at this point in these discussions, the military technologists enter with increasingly esoteric concern for technological balances, trade-offs, and counter-forces. This is quite problematical, for each participant deals in the worst-case assumptions about the capabilities and intent of the others. I recall, for instance, sitting in on a conference about the defense requirements of the Panama Canal. Before all of the possibilities had been exhausted, it was apparent that entire resources of the United States military establishment would be insufficient guarantee of the security of that single item. Given this sort of thinking, which is innate to the defense professions, it is hardly surprising that the negotiators not only failed then but that their discussions actually increased the sense of threat. It is in any case undeniable that the arms race has continued to spiral upward as more resources have been poured into efforts at restraining, capping, or reducing the levels. Indeed, the very concept of *disarmament*, as compared with arms restraint or reduction, is especially frightening, and I personally think that we should eliminate the use of the word. No one likes being helpless.

If direct approaches to the problems of arms buildups are nonproductive or even counterproductive, it is imperative that a search be made for other means of assuaging hurt feelings and reducing the fear of the other that invariably arises in circumstances of conflict. Then, perhaps, arms reduction will be achievable, for the nonrational drives for armaments will be reduced. In fact, the sort of experience that I described with armed and angry men *has* been duplicated in resolving disputes between groups of men and to some extent between nations. A new discipline of systematic nonforceful third-party mediation of disputes has emerged at the communal and international level in the past twenty years and already has demonstrated value in reducing the fear and anger in disputes that drive the need for weaponry. The disciplines are subject to refinement, but they are already professionally systematic and teachable as well as demonstrably effective in a great many cases. We still do not know the limits with any precision, but even these should change favorably as they become more widely institutionalized and recognized.

The aspiration for such peacemaking mechanisms is not new; it goes back at least to Isaiah, who called for men to reason together, some twenty-eight hundred years ago. It was still an aspiration when the UN Charter called on all parties to disputes to seek solutions through methods of negotiation, inquiry, mediation, conciliation, arbitration, judicial settlement, resort to regional agencies or arrangements, or other peaceful means in Article 33. It was an aspiration when the United States Arms Control and Disarmament Agency was established. It has been a great disappointment to the UN charterists that Article 33 has been much more honored in the breach than in practice. The fact is, no one knew quite how to go about realizing the noble concepts. It has caused despair to the legislators of the ACDA bill that that agency almost completely failed to develop any real capacity for peacemaking as was envisioned and became an arm of strategic negotiation, perhaps stimulating the arms race as much as restraining it.

When President Eisenhower made his farewell remarks, he had no concept of how "our peaceful methods and goals" could be carried out, except for his strong belief in direct contact between peoples. The idea existed, but not the method or the machinery. However, by the time President Carter took office a short sixteen years later, there were methods and there were some beginnings of institutions. And, although the Congress has entertained over one-hundred and forty bills embodying the aspiration since 1945, it was not until 1976 that substantive discussions and hearings could be held on the subject of how, practically, the aspiration could be achieved in reality. For the first time in history, a new instrument, a new social invention, has become available to and understood by a Congress and a president of the United States.

The central social invention, of course, is that of impartial honest brokerage of disputes. The invention has grown out of response throughout the developed Western nations to the crises of administrative legitimacy of the 1960s and 1970s; a response represented practically in the appearance and training of impartial mediators and dispute settlers who enter circumstances of conflict without force or power and engage in kinds of discussion with all the disputants on all the issues between them. These discussions often lead them to bring their differences to the negotiating table, where the mediators assist them in finding agreements between themselves, taken in their own self-interest, so that resulting agreements win essential values for all the participants.

Internally, in the Western nations, such methods have proven effective in conflicts and disputes in communities, between races, in schools, universities, and prisons, and between terrorists and governments. Internationally, these methods have been less often applied. But in well-documented cases in Cyprus and the Dominican Republic, they have contributed signally to conflict resolution. Equally important, these processes have been the subject of disciplined study by scholars, especially sociologists and social psychologists, and quite precise theories and languages have grown up to describe them. This development permits systematic description and provides basic tools for training and for research, for finding what works and what doesn't, why the procedures may sometimes fail or succeed, what the limits of usefulness are, when the methods are best mobilized in the course of a conflict cycle, and the like.

This new scientific discipline of deliberate conflict resolution is sufficiently advanced and sufficiently tested to move to the next step, that of institutionalization in training and research centers. This will provide cadres of professionally competent conflict resolvers who can enter both internal and international conflicts of nations without threat, force, or power and can facilitate persons coming to reason together without violence. Such institutions must be sufficiently visible and sufficiently legitimate functions of the national state, so that they will be called upon and used with regularity. You may recall that it was the police who called on me to talk with armed and angry men at a military post; similarly, professional soldiers such as General Andrew Goodpaster, the superintendent of West Point, endorse the Peace Academy idea.

Here, a crucial distinction of role must be clarified. The role of the conflict resolver or team can have no taint of advocacy. It is the essence of the social invention that the mediator establishes his position outside of the conflict system; he cannot be aligned with any party. He represents no interest other than nonviolent solution of disputes. This is entirely distinct from the diplomat whose role is representation of some sovereign interest. One element of the step of institutionalization is to establish such roles as legitimate, much as the Red Cross has established its symbol as a source of disaster relief. I look forward to the day when the arm band of the impartial mediator will be instantly recognized and will bring relief to those in unwanted disputes from which they cannot escape.

Now, what steps can accomplish this end of providing fear-reducing and anger-assuaging roles and mechanisms at communal and international levels. I suggest the following:

1. At the level of the national state, the establishment of academies of peace and conflict resolution to extend research and to train peacemakers who can nonviolently intervene in internal and external disputes with the acceptance of the parties to quarrel. The process of establishing such an institution is moving rapidly in the United States and is being considered in other countries, especially Canada, Mexico, United Kingdom, Holland, and Yugoslavia. Once national governments understand and trust the process, they are certain to welcome international mediative interventions in their own disputes.

2. At the international level, the establishment of a working international mediative service, much on the model of the Red Cross–Red Crescent Organization. A world conclave on this subject can be called within two years, and the organization can be so constructed as to be co-opted by the United Nations when functional usefulness is adequately trusted. The International

Peace Academy has made some beginning in this direction and would certainly represent a starting point.

3. Even now, the groundwork can be laid in the United Nations by action of the Security Council or General Assembly, or both, creating permanent committees on implementation of Article 33 concerning the peaceful settlement of disputes and temporary commissions to make definitive studies of the new developments and potentialities of the field.

These three steps are all attainable within less than five years, and the process will have begun.

Rather than attempting to predict how the arrangements may be made and carried out in any detail, I would like to visualize the possible outcome a decade from now, or, better yet, by the end of the century.

To start with one country, I can readily visualize a full-scale educational academy in place, with a focus on the training of peacemakers or impartial mediators and with a full panoply of research and analysis capacities at the graduate and professional level, all studying the causes and conditions of peaceful relations. Peace, here, is certain to be visualized as a condition in which normal and inevitable conflicts, quarrels, and disputes are conducted with a minimum of military or police violence. In the United States, I visualize a cadre of perhaps 200,000 such conflict resolvers placed through the society and carried on the public payrolls as social overhead. This, however, will prove to be a great saving, as both military costs and manpower and internal police forces will be reduced by 25 percent; that is, over 500,000 fewer military personnel and 600,000 fewer police officers will be needed to maintain the public order. All of the general officers and leading law enforcement officials with whom I've spoken agree that this is quite reasonable and very welcome; they resent the misuse of their forces for other than professional enforcement functions and believe that they would be relieved of unwelcome tasks to considerable degree. The savings would run in the neighborhood of $50 billion a year in current terms.

At the world level, I think that by the end of the century there would be a reliable cadre of mediators that would be called upon in many international disputes, perhaps first with the modest border quarrels that so often cause national mobilizations. As the process of fear reduction and the diminishing of hurt and angry national feelings takes hold, the pressure for armaments would be strikingly reduced; I have no difficulty supposing that a world savings of $100 billion a year in arms and military costs could be achieved and that the nations would actually feel more secure rather than less secure. Presumably, similar savings would be made in reductions of internal police forces.

What I cannot visualize, in the next century, at least, is any radical disarmament or dismantling of police and military forces; these will certainly continue, presumably in cooperative relations with the mediative process. Moreover, the diplomatic services would be even more active as the negotiators for the interests of the sovereignties that they represent; for, the end point of effective mediation is to bring disputes to the point of negotiation and disputants to the negotiating table, where the diplomats fulfill their proper roles as advocates.

In summary, arms reduction will, in the final analysis, depend fundamentally on reducing fear and anger in conflicting parties. New alternatives to resolve conflicts have been invented and are available for refinement and application at every level of society.

I would appeal to those persons and organizations who seek reduction in arms and conditions of peace in the world to work directly and earnestly for the establishment of national and international peace institutions, which can bring a balance and meshing of order-keeping forces and mechanisms with the processes of conflict resolution.

13
Discussion

Bryant Wedge: I'd like to make some semi-provocative comments on the things that have been said before in our symposium. I think most of us are not aware of something I think is happening—a really massive perceptual shift that can be said to be a paradigm shift, which is going on very widely, about the whole function of military power in relation to security. It is not just in this room, and we are not far out. Half the farmers in Iowa are ahead of us in recognizing this. The comments I want to make about the foregoing discussions, though, relate to the statement of Charles Osgood, who sees as one of the needs a decrease in the relative power of the national states accompanied by relative increase in the power of world government or the United Nations. I couldn't disagree more. My personal hope is that the United Nations becomes a less powerful organization, but a more effective one. Perhaps, as I discuss this matter further in some of my thoughts, it will become clear why I would say this. One of our grave problems in the world is the way it is organized in the hierarchies of power and the effect that this has on our thinking.

Power is the capacity, I think, to make other people do what they would rather not do, by force or threat of force. And that's exactly what I would not like to see the United Nations acquire more capacity to do, because whatever solutions are imposed on disputing or warring parties, in my view, the imposed solutions have the difficulty of there being some degree of losers on one or both sides. Whenever you have a loser, you have a sorehead, and the conflict cycles tend to go on. So the uses of power in solving problems are somewhat limited unless balanced, as I'll try to be quite clear, by mechanisms—which I think should be straightforward in the United Nations—that bring non-power, or what I call "zero power," solutions to conflict circumstances.

Jerry Frank I couldn't agree with more, when he says we are in the grip of forces of habit. You hear it at this table. One of the bad habits I would like to speak about is the use of the word "disarmament," which I think is a semantic trap of the worst kind. We use the word habitually. We don't mean "disarmament" at all. Some of us hope for an arms reduction, and when we say "disarmament" that's what we mean. But disarmament is one of the more frightening ideas that you can impose upon a person or a group of people. The use of the words actually, I believe, is one of the sources of resistance to negotiations to reduce arms, or what is called a "disarmament process." I don't think it should be called that. Every nation feeling in some degree a threat uses the image of being weak or disarmed in order to mobilize its population or people. Stalin said, "Mother Russia beat down and tramped in the mud." Lyndon Johnson said, "The United States cannot be a pitiful and weak giant." Hitler used images, not of strength, but of the terrors of weaknesses, to justify the organization of armaments. It is one of our semantic traps. I would be as careful about not using the word "disarmament" as I try to be careful about not using the word "chairman." I now speak of "chairperson" whenever I can think of it, because it offends certain people. I think words can be very important, and that the word "disarmament" actually presses the arms race a little bit the more we talk.

It's not lost on anybody that twenty-five years of talks on disarmament have been accompanied by a complete, thorough, steady, and unstoppable rise in the level of armaments. And there may be a correlation. I think there is.

Some time ago, I came to a commitment to take personal responsibility for ending war as a human institution: "I, Bryant Wedge, am going to end war as a human institution." And I know that Robert Muller took exactly the same kind of position when he found that twenty young Germans, of the teenagers whom he'd offered safe conduct, got killed by his *Maquis* pals. And he said right then, "This is insane. I am going to personally commit myself to end war and seek peace." I think one has to make that kind of commitment to begin work in the field. And I think we all have it. I think every person here has it.

The second thing that Jerry said that I liked particularly was a recognition of a need for new kinds of institutions. And I say this because I spent nearly twenty years trying to work through the established institutions, including this one, the United Nations, many times with the Palestine Conciliation Commission, or with one or another subcommittee, or with John Stoessinger's United Nations Study Group, and I worked with nearly every agency in the United States government in the foreign policy establishment—Arms Control and Disarmament Agency being one of them; a hopeless case. By the time it was three years old, it was captured entirely and co-opted by the establishments of military, intelligence, and technological minds. And these are very interesting minds. I was invited to come there as a behavioral scientist, and it could be nothing but a disaster because the co-optation was so strong that you had to work within a set of assumptions that were already established in that agency, which was a great disappointment to the legislators who set it up. Senator Pell said in our hearings, when Jerry Frank was there, that he was very dubious about a national peace academy notion; that we were pressing forward because of the fate of the arms control agency, which was taken over and co-opted by the habits of mind that said "power is king, and the capacity to organize power is what we are going to talk about, and our exchanges are going to be in this range." That is why I welcome this kind of conference, which particularly allows us a new venue, a new institution as a base to discuss this kind of matter.

I spent time before the National Security Council all during the Vietnam war, three or four trips, talking to groups of behavioral scientists, and they had to listen to us. But given the assumptive world that we are working against, we could make only the most modest of changes. What do you do when you have got thirty billion dollars and 500,000 men out there engaged in action? How do you really change these things? The differences or changes could only be marginal. We needed new institutions that don't work in that assumptive world.

Now, Dr. Spek, I would like to say that right now there is a lot of discussion. My brother happens to make some of these laser beam weapons. He is an advanced systems research project engineer, and he has been trying to "GRIT" it. These are not invented yet; they are on the drawing table. They are only potential, these laser beam weapons. He said that we could agree to stop at this level quite easily. It is very expensive to build these things, and they will be quite dangerous when we get them. It is perfectly clear that when one side does it, the other side will do it, and we worsen the whole circumstance without getting anything out of it. He and some other people are attempting to put a cap on that thing before it is built, stopping potential things before they are developed. That's a new feeling and atittude among arms designers.

The other thing I wanted to mention to you is that there is a group called War Control Planners. You may know Howard Kurtz in Washington, who takes this kind of message to congressmen, with little slide shows, very regularly and talks about the peaceful uses of outer space. His materials are very well developed and very well received. I said at the beginning that we were in the midst of a very large perceptual shift, and as a proof absolute of this, I want you all to carry a copy of this paper away with you: it says, "Congress passes peace academy commission bill." This is an extraordinary event because there have been two hundred years of efforts to establish a commitment on the part of our country, even before it was a great power, toward a peace-seeking process and to peacemaking activities. It was started by George Washington. It was outlined in a plan for a peace office in 1793 by Benjamin Rush. It was put forward in the Congress 140 times since 1935, in one form or another—departments for peace, institutes for conflict resolution, and so forth; and they all died at the hands of congressmen and senators on both sides of the aisle, by the way.

Something radical had happened, because by 1976, the Bicentennial year when this started to be put forward again, a young legislative assistant began to mobilize a few people to talk about this sort of thing. He talked to Jerry Frank, he talked to me, and we said it doesn't sound very practical because we tried so many times. But we began to talk to a few senators and congressmen, and found there was indeed some receptivity for this kind of notion; that we might establish in a great power, for the first time in history, an office dedicated to developing instruments for peacemaking and for monitoring the peace processes in the world, and the apparatus of scholarship which would then have access into the foreign policy process.

Robert Muller is quite wrong when he says that social sciences haven't done anything. They have done a great deal, amounting to a massive accumulation of evidence, tens of thousands of pieces of work in a number of fields. What has happened is that it hasn't gotten to Mr. Muller's attention, because there is no channel of access to him for this kind of material; it all has to pass through the established channels, and the established channels block this out.

We are trying to establish in the United States a peace office. Since 1976 a number of us have mounted a campaign, a public campaign, to establish a national academy for peace and conflict resolution, an educational institution analogous to war colleges in this country. When we started, I might say, every political wise person said, "That's absolutely impossible. This is a war-minded Congress and a war-minded country, and they will never go for it." Two years later 90 senators voted for, and none against, and 439 congressmen voted for, and 18 against—for whatever reasons, we don't know; they were radical rightist, every one of them, and did not want a spending bill. So the Congress—the Senate and the House—were quite educable to this fairly radical idea that we needed an institution at the federal level which, it is understood, will be independent or quasi-independent from the present foreign policy establishment and would provide channels of access for this kind of thinking and social science thinking at the highest levels of the government. It was then signed into law by Mr. Carter on November first of this year. So this is a landmark success. I believe it is a turning point and something very important.

What is the paradigm shift? What is going on in the people's heads, the congressmen's heads, that makes this possible? I think there is a general, very general understanding of just what we have been saying here—that is, the low payoff of any efforts to increase security through strength. To us it almost seems new, even though we have been supporting it for twenty or thirty years. But what is new is that this is very widely understood in the country, and it is understood by country preachers, and it is understood by rural congressmen, and it is understood by leaders including the President of the United States— who, incidentally, on page 121 of his book called *Why Not the Best?*, discusses a problem which he had when he became governor of the State of Georgia. He found that 47,000 man-hours and a good deal of equipment of his state police in Georgia were being utilized to suppress community conflicts, mostly racial community conflicts. And he installed a new little institution—a three man team of black and white policemen out of uniform who, when a community conflict began to arise and hit the newspapers, would go to the place and talk to each side and see if they could find some resolution without bringing the state police. He reports that 211 man-hours of state police time were spent in his last year of office. The costs benefits were immense. He reduced this wear and tear on the state police from 47,000 to 211 man-hours over a four-year term of office, and he attributes this to the simple device of a very cheap three-man team going around and talking to both sides.

This president understands this process, and I can tell you his ambassador to the United Nations particularly understands it, as he is a leading scholar of that field. What is the field? The field is the wide area of non-power, third party intervention in disputes or mediation of disputes.

Two things have happened. There has been the perception that you cannot claim security by arms or force or threat of force. It's no longer having the utility that it is supposed to have. It's kind of a last-ditch thing. And the second thing is that discoveries have been made indicating that it is possible in some cases, or even quite often, to bring parties who are in severe and even violent disputes into discussions with each other of such a kind that they begin to resolve the issues between them without violence. This has happened in many areas. I suppose the prime example is in the labor-management field, where we had armed labor wars in the twenties and thirties and a large number of people were killed. Now a federal mediation and conciliation service comes to intervene, and a system called "collective bargaining" has come out of it. The only problem is that labor and management now combine and rip off the rest of us. It has been altogether too successful. We don't kill each other in labor wars anymore; it's gone.

What happened, though, is that the crisis of legitimacy in the sixties in this country, and in other countries in the Western world, threw up a great many people who learned by doing, who jumped into the middle of things and became third-party intervenors without even knowing what they were doing to begin with. You'll think of the picture of Martin Luther King and his rabble marching up to a bridge, and Bull Connor with his police holding the bridge, and this little man John Doer from the United States Department of Justice, one man alone, walking between them and negotiating a free passage across this bridge. It happened again and again. It happens in prisons and in schools. It happens in communal conflicts. As it happened, a very disciplined, regular set of rules emerged which turn out to be teachable; so we now have trained in this country maybe two hundred professional level, third-party interveners, zero-power mediators, honest brokers who intervene in these kinds of conflicts. I can tell you stories about this every day. I am often involved in them.

One of the immediate problems is to search for who is a proper mediator. When the police are smart enough to stay away and contain the area, they've learned. They are sophisticated in Washington: they don't go in with guns; teams are mobilized first to try to find out what these people want, what are their demands, why are they doing it, and who they are. In one case, a radical Moslem group was holding 134 hostages at gunpoint. A team was mobilized to look for the proper mediator. What person can be acceptable both to the authorities and to these people? There was a telepone network going across the country, and we talked to Muhammad Ali among others, reaching very hard for the kinds of persons who could be credible and acceptable to both sides and carry on discussions.

As we were doing this, the word got out that we were looking for some honest brokers. The ambassador from Egypt called up the White House and asked if he could be of help. And as a matter of fact, everybody recognized immediately that we had found the perfect person acceptable to both sides. As an ambassador from a foreign country, we couldn't repudiate any agreement he made; he was from an Islamic country and had to deal with people subscribing to radical Islamic ideals. So both sides would believe him. Then it had to be set up very carefully. I am mentioning these things because there are technologies in the process. Arrangements had to be made so the ambassador could be sent in but be safe. You had to protect him from being shot, so there had to be backup systems of police, signaling systems, and all kinds of things to get him out alive if we sent him into these buildings and it blew.

In that case, we were able to shift that dispute from confrontation with guns into the courts. And strangely enough, the radical Moslem group was rather satisfied by the attention they got in the courts, even though they lost their cause. They refused certain defenses—insanity type defenses or group-insanity type defenses that might have saved them—because that is not what they wanted. They wanted to get a message across, and they got their primary message across and used the courtroom for that.

That sort of thing happens very often. Nowadays, and suddenly, this new technology has appeared. And it has also become academic. A few people have been out there studying what has happened. Notably, John Spiegel from the Brandeis Center for the Study of Violence, when it was alive, made a massive study of what happened in the 1972 conventions that kept it from blowing apart. It's 1,200 pages and, I hope, about to be published. Another is a sociologist who took his Harvard Ph.D. in the movements and strikes and sit-ins in the South, named James Laue, who is the co-chairperson of the National Peace Academy campaign. The deputy mayor of New York, Basil Patterson, has run for some years the Institute for Mediation and Conflict Resolution in New York City, which has dealt with the garbage strikers, the police strikers, and so forth, and probably did as much as anything to keep New York City viable.

Thus, there are people who have worked out some strong academic paradigms, and the strongest element in this is a greater appreciation of the roles of persons involved in conflict. Very quickly, there are the activists—the ones who want something—and their counterpart, the reactivists—the ones who try to keep them from getting it—who are threatened by it. Secondly, there are the advocates, the people who gather around activists; they may be lawyers or diplomats, whose only job is to negotiate in the interest of the sovereign. A diplomat should know what his job is, but they often get confused and think they are peacemakers. But they can't perform as such, because they represent sovereignties and they represent interests. Or they may be military, which are used to advocating a cause.

The third range of roles involving conflict—this is Laue's model—are enforcers; that is, people who can be brought in from outside to muffle a conflict, such as the peacekeeping forces in Lebanon, Cyprus, Sinai, Northern Ireland, which are enforcement mechanisms. And those are the three main mechanisms that sustain peace in the world today. There are two new ones which I call your attention to. One of them, I have spoken about. This is the impartial mediator, which, in the international scene, is very slowly beginning to appear.

I once worked with such a mediator in the Dominican Republic in 1965— paid for by the State Department, but given complete license to repudiate them or do anything I wanted to do. I was able to walk through our troops, 28,000 of them, and talk to the radical revolutionaries who were pent up behind them, and find out something that they wanted: a university. And then, by bringing a bunch of professors and papal nuncios and Mexican ambassadors into the scene, and finding a place where we could talk together, we were able to arrive at an understanding that the United States would support them in having a university center; that they wouldn't need to fight anymore, because they could turn to study in order to legitimize their reformist revolutionary aims. Thus, these principles can be applied internationally, and have even been systematically a few times.

Now, I want to go to the disarmament question. I'll go to the end of it by saying that, in my judgement, if we move in institutionalizing the mechanisms for dispute settlement, as I think is entirely possible—I am talking about attainable things—by the end of the century we can really have reduced the arms levels, the military costs worldwide, by 25 percent—a great saving. I'll tell you precisely which institutions I think are attainable quickly that would have this effect. Twenty-five percent is $100 billion in current terms. That $100 billion is only $25 for every man, woman, and child that we would be saving. The other $75 they would still be spending. Today, we are spending $100 for every man, woman, and child alive. In many countries, including China, $100 is greater than the individual share of the GNP. So it is a substantial thing. The savings are larger because as peace comes, the internal security forces—which are now, in this country and in other countries, almost as large as our military forces—those policemen, guards, and so forth at the door of every house and gate, executive protection services, would also decrease by about 25 percent.

Now you might think that the empires of the law enforcement officials and the military would not like this. And I have to tell you that they love the idea. Andrew Goodpaster, for example, who is our strongest general at the present time and the superintendent at West Point, tells us he advocates it and he does not mind being cut back 25 percent. He says that the army and military are being sent out to do things they shouldn't be doing. He said, "Fine, we're being used to try to resolve disputes by force which really are better resolved elsewhere, and we don't like it." And they don't mind at all the idea of having a more professional, a more elegant military-enforcement function.

I want to turn a little bit to the dynamics of the disarmament problem. When I worked with the Arms Control Agency in 1963, and it was already over the hill, I spent a good deal of time among the economists, military men, and strategists about this kind of language that Mr. Spek is talking. It turned out that they were deeply involved in the fine esoteric points of strategic balances—and they can get very esoteric, indeed, and very specialized. The specialism got more and more in the hands of these specialists. Now, the specialists are very funny, because they always work in terms of worst-case assumptions. And the question is, "What *if* they should develop X weapon?" or, "How would it affect the balance if somebody installed a few shelters, passive defense systems, or a few active defense ABM antiballistic missile systems?" It became very esoteric. And as they did it, they scared themselves to death. Worst-case assumptions in the hands of technologists are absolutely frightening. And by the time they talk to their political masters, they really become frightening. One of the outcomes, I believe, of the arms-control discussions has been to frighten people even more than ever. And what do you do when you are frightened? You increase your armament level. So fear is in there.

Fernando Lay: In our view, achievement of disarmament depends in large measure upon providing alternative methods for resolving differences, which allay, instead of engendering fear—methods which have been proven elsewhere in society. The development of a general treaty on models for peaceable solutions of disputes has been advocated by the delegation of Italy a number of times, and as recently as a few months ago when a certain proposal coming from the opposite side was treated in another committee. I refer to the Non-use of Force in International Relations. We wanted to take the other side of the coin, namely, to develop some binding methods for the solution of peaceful disputes.

These are tentative thoughts, which are in line with what I said yesterday on the need to stress the individual—the problems of individuals—especially since we are mainly devoting our attention here to the global dimension, to globalism. My few thoughts will try to present a quick, almost instant interpretation of the condition of modern man. Man first emerged as the least well equipped for the fight for survival. As a matter of fact, he was the weakest animal on earth. Yet he developed a capacity for imagination and thought which was the basis for transforming nature and himself. For many thousands of generations, man experienced himself as a child, dependent on nature, on fertility, on practically everything that surrounded him.

However, he slowly evolved and set himself a new goal—that of being free, of being fully human. Today, when man seems to have reached the beginning of a new, richer, happier human era, his existence and that of generations to follow is more threatened than ever. How is it possible? Man has, as many speakers have already stressed, almost achieved mastery over nature. He has won freedom—the freedom from political and secular authorities, but not the freedom to be himself. How does this happen? Perhaps it is due to his obsessive search for ever-increasing material comfort. Happiness seems to become identical with consumption of new items and better commodities. The value of man as a person seems to lie in his fallibility, not in his human qualities of love, reason, or in his artistic capacities. I hope this does not sound too European, since most of you are Americans. But man seems to be incapable to appreciate life, and unfortunately, is just ready to destroy everything.

Two great powers, as a matter of fact, two superpowers, have developed in this century. Being afraid of each other, they seek security in an ever-increasing military armament. Both rivals claim that their system promises final salvation for man. However, there is at the least a slight difference between the two systems. In our world, the Western World, there is freedom to express ideas critical to the existing systems. Hence, the Western World carries within itself the possibility for peaceful, progressive transformation. However, both systems are materialistic in their outlook in the long term. What are the prospects for the future, then? The most likely possibility is that of a nuclear holocaust. But even the avoidance of a nuclear war does not promise a bright future. I am afraid that the current process will proceed: more machines that act like men, and production of men who act like machines—an ever-increasing material power at the disposal of men without the wisdom to use it. So it is definitely not an encouraging prospect. I don't have a definite answer. Perhaps we must take responsibility for the life of all men and develop on a global scale what the developed countries have already developed internally—a relative share of wealth, a more just division of economic resources. Above all, there is a need, I think, to give human proportion to work and to promote a cultural renaissance. However, no change should be brought about by force; it should be a simultaneous one in the economic, political, and cultural spheres. What I am advocating is a new beginning; that is, to put man's power in the service of life and not in the service of death. I think we must choose life. And as long as we can consult together as we are doing in this room, we can hope and we are not lost.

Morton Deutsch: I would like to see if we could spend a little more time discussing what I think is an important issue in this area and which to some extent I disagree with: the comments that Bryant made about the resistance to change, the built-in vested interests which resist the process of reducing arms and bringing the armaments race under control. I think there are psychological processes and social processes involved, and unless these kinds of processes are well understood, we will continue to experience the sense of frustration and failure. I think that's a very central issue.

Ambassador Hoveyda: I would just say in one minute that the main issue, in my opinion, in the field of disarmament is the problem of the larger powers. If they give the example, then it would be very difficult for the smaller states not to follow them in that field. And *they* have to do it.

I don't think that they are arming because they fear each other. I don't think that they are arming because they want to sell arms. They can very well produce something else and sell it. What is much more important is the fact that each superpower practically has to ensure the future of a large portion of the world. And then interests develop, and these interests existed before superpowers. They continue to exist now, and they are following policies in order to keep their interests.

In fact, we are not in a committee of the UN. We are not representing our countries; we are just representing ourselves. So let's be very frank. In fact, we are arming, and armaments exist because somebody wants to take something from somebody else. Let's be very frank. We have to solve this problem if we want to end up with a real disarmament. And I agree with Professor Wedge on the fact that let's begin at home. Let's try to solve conflicts. Let's try to have more social justice and freedom inside our countries. That would help very much to ease tensions. And then, as they say, charity begins at home. Then let's see if we can develop something on the international scene.

Part IV
Alternative Mechanisms for Guaranteeing Peace and Security

14
Remarks by
Ambassador Piero Vinci

I would like to welcome my friends who have come together here once again to promote the cause of disarmament, and in particular General Romulo, one of the founding fathers of the United Nations. I have had the great privilege of being associated with this outstanding statesman on many occasions both inside and outside of the UN, benefiting each time from his political foresight and vision.

I would also like to make a few remarks as a token of gratitude to the organizers of this important colloquium, and especially to my good friend Donald Keys, president of the Planetary Citizens.

As General Romulo has stated so eloquently, disarmament is unthinkable without a new system of international security. It follows that the setting up of an effective system of collective security in accordance with the UN Charter is part of our first order of business. To achieve this far-reaching objective, a great deal of work must be accomplished.

The extreme difficulty of halting a continuing global arms race, this mad race—as U Thant called it—which is already absorbing an incredible quantity of human and material resources, requires, in my own view, a new approach, a mental approach adequate to our time. For this reason, especially for this reason, I found the subject of this colloquium particularly timely and significant.

Looking for a moment at the behavior of modern society in this context, what is most striking to me is the anachronism of current political thinking. While the scientific and technological revolution is running at supersonic speed, politics are proceeding at the pace of a horse-drawn carriage. In fact, we have not yet succeeded in liberating ourselves, in international affairs, from outmoded concepts of power politics and national egoism, which are more or less the same as those existing in the Stone Age; concepts which, in turn, are increasingly nourished by deeply entrenched negative forces such as fear, suspicion, mistrust, and self-interest. They are present everywhere and lie behind most of the current disputes or conflicts between nations. A case in point is the relationship between the two superpowers. Throughout its history, Russia has been surrounded and attacked by hostile forces, and has developed—understandably enough—a feeling of mistrust toward the outside world. This has led the Soviet Union to build up its military strength and enter into competition with the United States. America, on the other hand, which had never aimed at ruling the world, has been brought by the circumstances of history, and not by its own choice, to a dominant economic and political position. Ambition, which is a human instinct, has worked on both sides to raise the level of competition with all that has followed. The time has come to change all this: to free ourselves of these ancestral complexes of mistrust and suspicion, to speak openly and to stop trying to conceal what is in the back of our minds and what, at present, mass media disclose to the whole world.

I am convinced that only by using a new international language and by replacing mistrust with respective confidence, by adopting a global vision, can we face the global challenges of our time and start building a disarmed, peaceful, secure, and more just world.

15

Requirement for Alternative Mechanisms for the Maintenance of International Peace and Security under Progressive Disarmament

Alessandro Corradini

In the declaration contained in the Final Document of the Tenth Special Session of the General Assembly, the member states of the United Nations recognized that disarmament, relaxation of tension, respect for the right to self-determination and national independence, the peaceful settlement of disputes in accordance with the Charter, and the strengthening of international peace and security are directly related to each other; and that progress in any of these spheres has a beneficial effect on all of them, while, in turn, failure in one sphere has a negative effect on others. The members of this organization also recognized that there is a close relationship between disarmament and development, and that progress in the former would help greatly in the realization of the latter. Therefore, resources released as a result of the implementation of disarmament measures should be devoted to the economic and social development of all nations and contribute to the bridging of the economic gap between developed and developing countries.

In the Program of Action, the membership agreed that progress in disarmament should be accompanied by institutions for maintaining peace and the settlement of international disputes by peaceful means. In particular, during and after the implementation of the program of general and complete disarmament, adequate measures should be taken to maintain international peace and security, including the obligation of States to place at the disposal of the United Nations agreed manpower necessary for an international peace force to be equipped with agreed types of armaments, so as to ensure that the United

Nations can effectively deter or suppress any threat or use of arms in violation of the purposes and principles of the United Nations Charter.

I believe that, while these declaratory statements do not exhaust the problem we are dealing with, they contain the basic elements of the problem, as the United Nations has consistently viewed it during all the years of its existence.

I wish to recall, in this connection, the view of Secretary-General Hammarskjöld on the subject. On April 28, 1960, in addressing the Ten-Nation Disarmament Committee, he assumed that, at some stage, a study "will have to be made of those matters which are covered by Chapter VII of the Charter and which would become of crucial significance in case of progressive or complete disarmament."

Hammarskjöld also addressed himself to the question of how to fit the control activities relating to comprehensive disarmament into the organizational framework of the United Nations. In this connection, he thought, "The Organization has such possibilities of development and such flexibility that I do not foresee any difficulties in fitting an activity of this type into the United Nations framework in a way which would fully safeguard all legitimate interests involved."

Finally, he argued that essential difficulties encountered within the United Nations were based on political realities and not on the principles according to which the United Nations had been established or the mode in which it was organized. From this he drew the conclusion:

> In the work for achieving and maintaining disarmament [essential difficulties] would not be experienced with less force were an attempt to be made to start, so to say, all over again; time will be gained and better results achieved if our efforts are developed with respect for what has been achieved so far and for the necessity of organic adaptation of these achievements to new needs within the framework of new possibilities.

The following year, 1961, in their Joint Statement of Agreed Principles for Disarmament Negotiations, the Soviet Union and the United States seemed to come very close to Hammarskjöld's assumptions.

Outlining the principles of new disarmament negotiations, the Soviet Union and the United States agreed on the following:

> The goal of [disarmament] negotiations is to achieve agreement on a programme which will ensure: (a) that disarmament is general and complete and war is no longer an instrument for settling international problems, and (b) that such disarmament is accompanied by the establishment of reliable procedures for the peaceful settlement of disputes and effective arrangements for the maintenance of peace in accordance with the principles of the Charter of the United Nations.
>
> All disarmament measures should be implemented from beginning to end under such strict and effective international control as would provide firm assurance that all parties are honouring their obligations. During and after the

implementation of general and complete disarmament, the most thorough control should be exercised, the nature and extent of such control depending on the requirements for verification of the disarmament measures being carried out in each stage. To implement control over the inspection of disarmament, an international disarmament organization including all parties to the agreement should be created within the framework of the United Nations. This international disarmament organization and its inspectors should be assured unrestricted access without veto to all places as necessary for the purpose of effective verification.

Progress in disarmament should be accompanied by measures to strengthen institutions for maintaining peace and the settlement of international disputes by peaceful means. During and after the implementation of the programme of general and complete disarmament, there should be taken, in accordance with the principles of the United Nations Charter, the necessary measures to maintain international peace and security, including the obligation of States to place at the disposal of the United Nations agreed manpower necessary for an international peace force to be equipped with agreed types of armaments. Arrangements for the use of this force should ensure that the United Nations can effectively deter or suppress any threat or use of arms in violation of the purposes and principles of the United Nations.

These principles were developed into concrete draft provisions by the Soviet Union in its "Draft Treaty on General and Complete Disarmament Under Strict International Control" of March 1962, and by the United States in its "Outline of Basic Provisions of a Treaty on General and Complete Disarmament in a Peaceful World" of April 1962.

The relevant provisions of the United States draft were particularly significant. In defining the guiding principles of its document, the United States made clear that, as national armaments were reduced, the United Nations would be progressively strengthened in order to improve its capacity to ensure international security and the peaceful settlement of differences as well as to facilitate the development of international cooperation in common tasks for the benefit of mankind. In other words, disarmament, verification, and measures for keeping the peace would proceed progressively and proportionately, beginning with the entry into force of the Treaty.

At the beginning of the first of the three stages of the disarmament process under the Treaty, an International Disarmament Organization (IDO) would be established within the framework of the United Nations. The IDO would verify the implementation of the envisaged disarmament measures in accordance with agreed principles. The Parties to the Treaty would also submit to the IDO reports on their military expenditures; would give advance notification of major military movements and manoeuvers; and would permit observation posts to be established at agreed locations, including major ports, railway centers, motor highways, river crossings, and air bases, to report on concentrations and movements of military forces. Moreover, the Parties to the Treaty would undertake obligations to refrain, in their international relations, from the threat or use of force of any type—including nuclear, conventional, chemical, or biological means of warfare—contrary to the purposes and principles of the United Nations Charter. Concerning the peaceful settlement of disputes, the Parties to the Treaty would utilize all appropriate processes for the peaceful settlement of all disputes which might rise between them and any other States (whether or not Parties to the Treaty)—including negotiation, inquiry, mediation, conciliation, arbitration, judicial settlement, recourse to regional agency or arrangement, submission to the Security Council or the General Assembly of the United Nations, or other peaceful means of their choice. The Parties would further agree that disputes concerning the interpretation or application of the Treaty which were not settled by negotiation or by the IDO would be subject to referral by any party to the dispute to the International Court of Justice, unless the parties concerned agree on another mode of settlement.

Even more important, the Parties to the Treaty would undertake to develop arrangements during stage I for the establishment in stage II of a United Nations Peace Force. To this end, the Parties to the Treaty would agree on the following measures within the United Nations: (a) examination of the experience of the United Nations leading to a further strengthening of United Nations forces for keeping the peace; (b) examination of the feasibility of concluding promptly the agreements envisaged in Article 43 of the United Nations Charter; (c) conclusion of an agreement for the establishment of a United Nations Peace Force in stage II, including definitions of its purpose, mission, composition and strength, disposition, command and control, training, logistical support, financing, equipment, and armaments. Finally, the Parties to the Treaty would agree to support the establishment within the United Nations of a Peace Observation Corps, staffed with a standing cadre of observers who could be dispatched promptly to investigate any situation which might constitute a threat to or a breach of the peace. Elements of the Peace Observation Corps could also be stationed as appropriate in selected areas throughout the world.

In the second and third stages of the disarmament process, further measures relating to reduction of the risk of war and the keeping and strengthening the peace would be taken.

I would like to stress one particular aspect of the provisions in the United States Outline on general and complete disarmament, and that is the following: the peacekeeping and peacemaking measures in the United States outline are viewed as being concomitant with and proportional to the disarmament measures to be carried out.

These two principles also found clear expression in the report of Secretary-General Waldheim on the relationship between disarmament and international security that he submitted to the Tenth Special Session. In considering how the twofold process of disarmament and strengthening of international security could be accelerated, the Secretary-General recognized that "at an advanced stage in the disarmament process, the adoption of further disarmament measures will become interwoven with the task of establishing and developing adequate machinery and procedures for keeping the peace and for settling disputes by peaceful means."

In the same vein, the Secretary-General spoke of a twofold task: "the cessation of the arms race and disarmament, on the one hand, and the building up of a system of world order based on collective responsibility, on the other hand."

Having referred to these views of the Secretary-General, I would like to stress that, as quoted above, he spoke of the twofold task as arising "at an advanced stage in the disarmament process." Indeed, in his report the Secretary-General clearly implied that some initial measures of disarmament could be safely taken, so to say, on their own merit. In his own words:

> Initially, armaments may be a symptom of underlying political differences, but beyond a certain point the armaments programs themselves, the apprehensions they cause . . . and the attitudes and institutions they give rise to, assume the character of independent forces propelling the arms race. In this situation, countries tend to view questions of international peace and security chiefly in terms of relationships of force and of military safeguards against any conceivable contingency.

In other words, "the arms race fosters the very attitudes and institutions which perpetuate it."

There can be no doubt, in this connection, that the spiraling arms race since the end of the Second World War has generated a momentum of its own, which can hardly be viewed as being commensurate with the underlying political problems.

I have spoken from an institutional viewpoint, and this will not come as a surprise, since I have spent more than two decades in the United Nations Secretariat, dealing with the problem of disarmament and also serving in some major United Nations peacekeeping operations. I am fully aware that there are many other valid approaches to the question of alternative mechanisms for the maintenance of international peace and security in a world that has set disarmament as one of its principal goals.

It should be possible, however, to reconcile the many approaches to the question, provided it is recognized on all sides that, first, there can be greater security for all states at a lower level of armaments and forces and, second, that a process of comprehensive disarmament, accompanied by effective international mechanisms for the maintenance of peace, is worth pursuing most vigorously, because the eventual result would be "an unqualified blessing to all mankind."

16

Discussion

Elise Boulding: I would like to tie in some of yesterday's and this morning's discussions with our subject this afternoon. In order to do so, I would like to introduce a concept that we have been working with this past week in Tokyo at the United Nations University: the concept, which Johan Galtung introduced, of "deep structures." Some of you know the term "deep structures" in a linguistic sense as Chomsky has used it. But this concept of deep structures is in a sociological sense, and if you respond to it intuitively that's the best way to respond to it: to understand how all of the structures at all levels of consciousness, values, behavior patterns, thinking, and social institutions all reinforce one another to produce certain kinds of behavior.

I'll mention very briefly some of these aspects of deep structures. The first one of them is language. The ways in which we use language shape what we see in the world as we speak about it. The fact is that all of the discussions around this table, as everywhere else, have been in terms of man and his world and mankind. While the intention is to speak about the human condition, the actual reality evoked inside our heads is that of men dealing with men. Therefore, quite unconsciously—there is no intention involved here—the deep structures of a certain set of roles associated with conquest domination and the hero—not the heroine, but the hero—are evoked as we are struggling to think about a peaceful world. The mental imagery that goes with that image comes complete with the words we use. The cultural expressions of them are found in drama, poetry, music, and art.

One can get a coherent picture that corresponds to these deep structures. We look at the instinctive responses of human beings—their culturally programmed responses. We look at patterns of interpersonal behavior. We look at political structures which are by and large status-oriented, and the prevalent status is the conquering male and everything that goes with it. We have great difficulty, incidently, with non-status actors, which are more like the children that Professor Markley was speaking of yesterday, because the non-status actors are allowed to be benevolent, kind, and cherishing, and maybe not quite so ambitious. We reserve a special place for certain kinds of humanist values; they are alright for women and children. That is part of our deep structure. In economic structures and family structures, there are certain things which are appropriate for male human beings to do, other things which are appropriate for female human beings to do. Also built into this is the

136

concept of what is alright for children, middle-aged people, and the elderly, and what is alright for minority races as compared to majority races.

All of these lie embedded right through every layer of the social reality we experience. When we talk about trying to "pull out" the values that can make for a peaceful order, we are talking about a very difficult process of pulling out values which are indeed there, but which are encapsulated in things that are alright for women and children to do. And we are talking about bringing them out into the public arena as behavior that is appropriate for people who have affairs of state to conduct, the people who have military decisions to make, people who have the affairs of multinational corporations to deal with. The values of altruism, nurturance, and sharing are certainly present in our society, but they are compartmentalized in those deep structures. The values of power, dominance, and assertiveness are also present, and they are available to us in the public mode that is the accepted mode for the conduct of public affairs.

I suggest that all of the consciousness movements, the self-awareness, the human potential movements, some of which may seem trivial, sentimental, or foolish, are all attempts to reexamine these deep structures; and it is hard to do so; some of the efforts look silly. But the effort to do it will in effect make possible the release of values that have been compartmentalized in some parts of these structures into the whole structure. And that is what I would say the consciousness raising and the holistic thinking of our time is all about, and what we in fact are trying to do. This has been a preface to more specific dealings with the conditions of disarmament.

I would like to say that the little dialogue between Robert Muller and David Singer—where the one was saying that disarmament is impossible but we must be looking at the larger processes, and the other was saying that there is nothing else to talk about; disarmament or nothing—very nicely expresses the dilemma that we are all dealing with. As for this thing which we are calling disarmament, I am willing to accept Bryant's suggestion that it may not be a good word, that we should be talking about nonviolent, nonmilitary dispute, settlement, or something. Part of the creation of the conditions for it is simply the assertion that this is happening. Let's not talk about the time frame in which it is happening, but simply assert that a demilitarized world is going to happen.

Unless that is part of our thinking, then our strategies are not very useful. Unless the image of that reality out there—twenty years, fifty years, a hundred years—is very clear in our minds, we have no plausible reason to continue. We can be optimistic, or pessimistic, but we have no plausible reason to continue. So it's not a pleading, *"Please let us disarm;"* it is an assertion, "This *will* happen." The appropriate language for it, I won't deal with, but whatever that thing is, which is a demilitarized world, is happening, and the task that we have is not to plead that it should happen, but simply to say: "Alright, it is happening. What are the most useful things of the various ones we could be doing to get on with the process?" That is a different way of asking the question, rather than simply saying, "What should we do to get disarmament?"

One of the things that I think is important, again in this contextual sense, is to stop talking about security. Almost all of the discussions, both in the written literature and the discussions here, have been struggling with "How can people feel secure?" The one thing we can be certain of is that we will have rising levels of insecurity for at least the next fifty years, at least, rising levels of insecurity for individuals, for families, for groups, for nations, for the world. The reasons for those, you have all spelled out, but you haven't said in so many words the logical inference of the statements you have made: We are facing rising levels of insecurity. Therefore, the demilitarization of the world must be in the context of rising insecurity.

That has always been the context in which the disarmaments of history have taken place. Some current examples would be Malaysia and Indonesia—fantastic insecurity, high levels of confrontation, mutual penetration of each other's borders with guerrilla bands, and so on. There was between them a steady de-escalation in the last ten years, in the face of rising insecurity, because there was a political decision that this had to happen.

We must look at the arenas where arms reduction is taking place. We are so transfixed by the bipolar superpower thing that we are looking in the wrong places for models of the process that we are concerned about. Between Canada and the United States, where we take for granted that there is total security, the agreement on the disarmament of the Great Lakes was arrived at in conditions of great tension, and the disarmament began under conditions of high tension, with a decision that there were no payoffs in it for the United States and Canada. Egypt and Israel, if they succeed in this round of efforts, are doing it under conditions of greatest insecurity. So let's stop talking about guaranteeing any country, large power or small power, security. It cannot be guaranteed. We face a world of rising insecurity; we acknowledge that; we acknowledge a world of uncertainty, and our problem is the management of insecurity and the management of uncertainty—the management of living with acute vulnerability.

What we do with that vulnerability now is to write worst-case scenarios. And I suggest a very specific strategy that should be required from now on of any strategist, of any person who is dealing with future scenarios in regard to arms or any other policy that has to do with the international arena: their assignment should be to write the best-case scenario. A very simple concept. You must always write the best-case scenario. What is the best thing that could happen as a result of this deployment of resources, of this particular program of action? And in the case of disarmament, once you start writing best-case scenarios instead of worst-case scenarios, and are committed to writing them and passing them around, they become part of the literature; they become part of the strategy discussions, and you have started a different dynamic. I am almost ashamed to even suggest the best-case scenario strategy, because it seems so simpleminded. But it is in fact the one thing that does not take place—at least as I read the literature.

I am very grateful for the introductory presentation because I didn't know whether we would have such a strong presentation, and I am very glad we did, of the institutional mechanisms. I am not going to speak of those, since you have done so, reminding us that they exist, giving us a very firm base to build on. I would like to suggest a systematic de-escalation of the importance assigned to the big powers. Just stop talking about them so much. I would say that our progress in disarmament will be measured by the decline in the number of references to the Soviet Union and the United States, because they continually deflect the actual kind of planning that needs to be made. I would say that we should be asking for disarmament strategies from the world cities, if I can borrow a leaf from Chad Alger's book. I want to know what Peking and London and Paris and New York and Rome can contribute in strategic terms to the lowering of arms levels. And I think they can contribute quite a lot.

The NGO world has, in one sense, been mobilized, but they are mobilized to be supportive. I want to know what responsibilities the NGOs in the labor-union field will take, what responsibility the NGOs for the world's professionals and the physical sciences and the social sciences will take. What will they take responsibility for? Instead of their simply saying, "We think you should do this" or "We think you should do that," we should say to them, "What will *you* do?" And this they are not being asked.

This will partly deal with what Dave Singer pointed out, I think very rightly, that it is very easy for scientists to be co-opted into their national defense systems. If they are in their NGO, transnational identity, held responsible for disarmament processes, then suddenly there is an input that reaches them directly; they cannot, at least unthinkingly, answer the invitation to go to London or to Paris or to Washington to deal with these things. So taking different groups and identifying what responsibilities they will take, I think, will be very helpful.

One thing about the world information order that can increase this process is the telematic revolution that hasn't really been discussed here. We've heard about one way; that is, TV and radio programs, and so on. The really significant change on the horizon in the next ten years is that we will be able to have two-way direct communication with any group on any part of the planet. Professionals can consult with each other, peace movements can consult with each other, town to town, village to village, with a level of sophistication of electronics equipment which we don't happen to have right now but is really, literally around the corner. This is very relevant to disarmament, because disarmament is encapsulated in a secrecy system, which cannot sustain itself once the telematic revolution is fully under way. No nation-states will be able to retain the levels of secrecy that they are now able to maintain. They will not be able to because there will be people who can decode anything that can be coded. Short of the horrifying thought of nuclear explosions which wipe out all communication equipment—and Mr. Spek, I am very grateful that you mentioned that because that is another thing to take account of—the communication access is a whole process which can further disarmament and which has not been mentioned.

Just one or two more things I want to suggest here. One is to begin to set a timetable for the standardization of arms; no more research on development of esoteric new weapons. NATO's arms should be standardized to where any part of any weapon can be made in any country and added to a weapon in any other country. This is the secret of the European coal and steel community: you had essentially a standardization of the industrial processes and you had a scrambling of the production system so that things no longer happened inside national borders. Once you standardize your product and scramble your production system, the whole business of military secrecy and breakthroughs in weapons has no meaning anymore. Now I realize that it is one thing to say this, and another thing to stop the process of diversification, but the ideas have to be there and they have to be asserted at the point where people can start seeing things differently. One thing we have all agreed on around this table is that there is a general awareness now of the absurdity of the arms race. That awareness should be harnessed to the fact of the possibility of standardization and scrambling. So to whatever extent people still feel that there is some security to be had in arms, at least this is an internationalized process, regionally. I don't expect NATO and the Warsaw Pact to scramble across the borders, but I would certainly expect NATO to scramble within its system and the Warsaw Pact within its system.

I should like to mention the development, which is provided for within the UN Charter, of regional security councils. This has not been done. The only one that really exists—if it can be called a security council, and I think it can—is ASEAN. Every region can be generating the regional military reduction strategy within its region away from the bipolar poles in a more task-oriented way, not continually deflected by big-power wishes. Most of the disarmament that has taken place already is of that nature; it is regional. So let's continue. Some of it is at a purely rhetorical level; anybody who thinks that the Indian zone of peace is anything more than words, of course, is a fool. On the other hand, there are some areas where that concept is not absurd. Letting each region do what it can, within the context that arms reduction is an absolute necessity, will free a lot of skills and strategies that are not now available because we try to do everything in the superpower context. And one thing that sociologists know is that small nations tend to be more innovative in foreign policy than large nations; they have less to lose. And so, by regionalization of disarmament, you are freeing the more creative and innovative capacities of small nations in the regional and, again, you are simply lessening the importance of the superpowers. John Burton's work on localism—that is, settling the conflict as close as possible to where it's really being generated—is completely dealt with by this concept of regionalism.

I don't need to say anything about the UN forces, because it has already been so well said. I would simply applaud and point out that we have not understood what it has meant that soldiers of any one of the world's armed forces have been able to enter the UN forces and behave as peace soldiers even though they were trained to fight. The fact that they can do so is quite extraordinary. Soldiers with very conventional military training wind up in Cyprus, and suddenly they can't have guns. To be a good soldier in that situation means operating in such a manner that there shall be no violence, that one shall not have to use a gun, that they must redefine the situation, and that they can be good soldiers and proud of being soldiers. It amounts to a redefinition of the concept of "soldier" into a peace-keeping role that we would have thought impossible; yet, operationally, this is happening. More use of that experience and more shifting of forces into settings where this becomes their behavioral mandate is one way of dealing with the demobilization, which no one has talked about. We have got an awful lot of people in armies, and using the UN Forces for that demobilization would be very useful. We should also study the policies of Costa Rica, Sri Lanka, and Finland. They are all in conditions of high tension with very dangerous borders around them; yet they have been able to face the world and have considerable pride and self-respect without armies. How has Canada, although it certainly has an army, been able to have a justifiable pride? How did that happen? Why aren't they embarrassed at their role? On the whole, I don't sense any embarrassment for Canada, at any rate.

What are the capacities for the peace-studies programs around the world, the International Peace Research Association here in North America, the Consortium on Peace Research, Education and Development, as well as the National Peace Academy of which Bryant spoke? What this means now—this development which has been taking place at least since the fifties and is expanding country by country—is that we now have the capabilities for new behavioral repertoires in situations of conflict: negotiation, talent, ideas; in other words, resources are building up to meet the consequences of the lowering of arms, meaning that there are going to be a lot of problems, a lot of conflicts to deal with. This development provides the sense of being empowered to deal with conflicts at the same time that one is reducing arms, so that one doesn't feel scared and defenseless.

These two factors must meet each other—the reducing of arms and the building up of a lot of skills. An intelligent use, in the UN and out of it, of all of these peace studies and peace training programs is crucially important. Finally, I want to point out that the kind of change we are facing, the threshold that we are on, does not simply require more skilled use of scientific capability— social science and physical science; it doesn't only require a little bit more empathy, a little bit more understanding, a sense of world community; it requires tapping a vein of the human condition that is not widely tapped, and that is the spiritual vein. Something of the spiritual nature of the human individual is present everywhere. So if we are talking of resources, that is the most universal resource we have. It isn't brought into play; it's left out. In our deep structures, the spiritual nature is in a little corner, well hidden. So, if we look in those deep structures, pull out the things that we have hidden—the nurturant, the caring, the spiritual, the altruistic, what's alright for women and children—and bring it into the public domain and release it there, and if we explore the various kinds of systemic and institutional approaches that others have mentioned and I have mentioned, then I think that we do have a chance. But it is a long process, and we shouldn't argue about whether it is possible in ten years or twenty years. We should simply make the commitment that it is going to happen and determine what our strategies are for dealing with it.

Saul Mendlovitz: We've been invited to think of software in regard to disarmament, so I am going to say something which is really well known to this group, sort of in my chairperson capacity of the Advisory Council of the Planetary Citizens organization. The proposition that I want to start with is that to think, feel, and act as a global citizen in all walks of one's life is the essence of achieving disarmament and a just world order. And to achieve disarmament, one will have to go far along the route to achieving a just world order. And the way to do that is through a global social movement. And I mean that as seriously as one means it when one is talking in Western civilization about Christianity and Communism. I mean that one has to identify throughout the globe, individuals in all walks of life, not just in the proletariat or in the elite or in the intelligentsia, but in all walks of life—individuals who by bad luck or good luck have been struck by the sociological , condition of interpenetration or by the spiritual condition of the solidarity of humanity.

Without that kind of notion, I frankly do not believe that we are going to get through the great transformation equivalent to the neolithic transformation. We are moving through that transformation, and whether we come out at the other end in anarchy, or as a tyrannical world state, is anyone's guess. The notion that we are going to arrive at some humanistic, what I would call humane, governance—just, participatory, humane governance—requires a cadre of individuals who have taken upon themselves, in their psyche and in their lifestyles, some kind of realization that they have common solidarity with other human beings throughout the globe, and multiple loyalties. You begin with the notion that somehow or other you are part of the human race and then that you are lucky to be born in Scranton, Pennsylvania, the United States, a Hassidic Jew, and a male.

I do not understand how we can really begin to talk seriously about something as significant as disarmament, global security arrangements, or insecurity without thinking through carefully how you get all the individuals who are not part of the elite structure, who did not eat at this luncheon and who will not be invited to this luncheon, some really definite segment of those people, involved in an enterprise in which they understand what they are doing whether in Goa or fifty miles outside of Lima, Peru.

If we are going to really serious about what we are about, we are talking about the establishment of a social movement for a just world order. In that vein, it seems to me, to get a little more concrete, we certainly want to redefine what we mean by sovereignty. The movement from neolithic to the territorially fixed agricultural unit, and all the way down to the industrial revolution to what I will now call the communicative, or cybernetic or interpenetrative, era—we are now moving into that era—calls for a redefinition of sovereignty. It may be the cities or it may be transnational groupings, or it may be classes—look at the number of people who want to join the middle class throughout the world. There must be that kind of breaking through the categories of the nation-state system to understand who it is that has what kinds of expectations on the territory you call Earth, and a realization that somehow or other you want now to identify with those people and expand the identity that they have. My feeling is that until we get those identity expansions to a large number of groupings throughout the world, all the kinds of things that we promote—and I no longer promote SALT II—such as international security forces and peace academies, seem to be meaningless, unless we have a new mythic structure, a new belief system, a new value orientation on the part of large groups throughout the world. I understand that this sounds like exhortation, but I mean it as a serious political project for wherever you are in any part of the world, so I go out and preach that sort of thing.

To put life into what I have said, it seems to me that it is obviously clear that, within that context, disarmament is one of the major elements that no one wants to look at; the diversion of resources, the notion that you can continue to achieve "security" with everybody increasing their armaments. There are certain people everywhere in the world who will understand that that is an irrational and ultimately a nonfunctional kind of system. But I guess I would add that in the argument between Muller and Singer, without having heard it, it sounds as though I come down on the Muller side.

Let me put it in another way. I believe that there is a system in the world that I would call global apartheid. And I don't mean it as a metaphor. I believe that if you look at the globe, you will see that it is set up in such a fashion that the whites of the world run it, that 20 percent of the world receives 70 percent of the world's income. And if you look at that globe, it is the brown and the black that do not participate either in the income or in the decision making with regard to it.

Any kind of a global social movement that doesn't attend to the global apartheid system is unlikely to bring in most of the other people of the world. Now, it is possible that the superpowers could impose a concert of the globe on the world. It is not unthinkable, and I take it that this is what the Trilateral Commission thinks is possible, or at least preferable if not possible, and that is why they are about that effort. In fact I would guess that the Nixon-Kissinger model of the pentagonal world with some deputies was precisely that kind of view. But if you feel as an ethical matter that that is an undesirable world and, as I happen to believe, that that is an unstable world which it will not remain with any viability, then you must go to a global social movement in which you are looking at apartheid at the global level as one of the foci that you are looking at for dismantling. Now if that is the case, then let me talk a little more closely about what looks like it's not disarmament at all, but what I consider to be very essential in achieving disarmament. If I could say what we would do, I would say that what we ought to do is to topple South African apartheid through international police forces. I would call the people who run that society criminals. And I would march in and try to apprehend them as criminals and try them for crimes against humanity, because one of the things that I feel is happening in the field of disarmament and security is that it is tied to peacekeeping in a most mechanical fashion: "Separate the combatants." As one who professes law but who believes that law is a value-realizing process— not merely a set of precedents which come down to be applied over a case, but one which is trying to achieve humane values—I believe that that society is much like in the "American Dilemma." Myrdal pointed out that creed and practice has now gotten so far out of line that we were now going to have to do something about it in this society—that a society run by those people is now an outlaw society, and if we really want to encourage the kind of security forces we need, we should align our security forces with justice, not merely peace-keeping.

I would select as a strategy, not merely the peacekeeping places of the world, but the places where there is an overwhelming consensus of the community with regard to the police going in and doing justice. I have a second point, again at the level of peacekeeping. I hope that if we pick up the peacekeeping, maybe it will take care of the disarmament aspect. My sense is that humanitarian intervention, when the Nigerians go into blood-letting, when the Burundis decide that they are going to kill themselves, or where you get a large-scale organized violence as in the Bangladesh experience, makes sense, if for no other reason than to set up a corridor where the people who don't want to get involved can at least go and be taken care of, and they will not be pillaged and raped and killed. My sense is that somehow that kind of global community process ought to be initiated again to destroy the myth structure of what?

The territorial fixed unit: that if you do something in your unit and it's your unit, well, we won't go in because it is domestic jurisdiction. We're not going to deal with that problem. This is a kind of moral insanity; a moral blindness at least. Again, it seems to me, that we should move, not in disarmament, but toward establishing security forces. I would advocate moving toward humanitarian intervention as a way of achieving what we are about.

So let me recapitulate. First of all, we all talk about where we came from. Elise just came back from the UN University. She has had this experience and she has heard the "manhood"—and I am glad she did it because it doesn't sound good coming from me—instead of the "personhood," and then she goes into the thing she has learned there. I happen to be teaching a course in the Ira Wallach Chair of World Order Studies at Columbia University this year. And I have been trying to operationalize to think, feel, and act as a global citizen. That is what I have been doing throughout the course, and it's an extraordinarily difficult kind of thing to do. How do you disaggregate what you mean by a global citizen? How do you do anything for the benefit of humanity? Force yourself to ask the question when you are looking at SALT II or a 20 percent decrease in the budget of the United States or deciding if Rumania is right or not right going into Comecon or not going into Comecon. What would the difference be if you were looking at that from a global perspective rather than looking at it from the viewpoint of an individual who is in a nation-state, the United States, asking himself the question, "Is this for the benefit of the United States?" "Can we sell it here?"—which is the "hard line." If you are a peacenik you ask yourself the question, "Can we sell it here?"

The question is, Can you sell it to yourself? That is the first question; Can you sell it to yourself and to other people around you? And I am arguing that we need a set of concrete political projects, like toppling apartheid in South Africa as the first step in toppling apartheid on the globe; like humanitarian intervention that would begin to develop the global social movement throughout the globe; that would then lead us toward the disarming process. Not, mind you, that I am opposed to efforts for disarmament. In fact, just in case you haven't heard about it, Bill Coffin is having a big symposium up at the Riverside Church this coming weekend on disarmament and conversion, and I am all for all of us joining in that conversion convocation and getting this society in the position where it understands that it is to its advantage to convert to civilian and peacetime. But I do think that, in doing that, it is very important that the mayors and the administrators and the clergy people who are brought there for that kind of convocation are bitten by that which bites most of the people who bother to come to this thing: that somehow they understand that they are part of a global community.

I've tried to state a few things that I think I would do—with apartheid and with humanitarian police forces. I would start to argue for the right to food on a global basis, with the duty of a global food force to feed us. We have started in the NIEO to talk about the automaticity of transfers; that means a global tax. I would certainly promote a global tax. We would talk about economic conversion in various societies and we would talk about transnational groupings. It seems to me that all of that is part of the essence of thinking and feeling and acting like a global citizen: starting where you are in initiating the global social movement, reaching first into your local community for those who are bitten, unlucky enough to be struck by global consciousness, and then finding a way that you can reach across what are called political boundaries to find the people on the other side. In that way, and the odds are like 1 in 200, we might achieve a disarmed world.

Bryant Wedge: This reminds me that I left something out. I said that there were five roles in conflict circumstances: that of activists, advocates, enforcers, and the two new roles which were barely being represented: those of mediators and partial mediators, and I left out the fifth, which is critical—the role of researcher. I am reminded because I have heard between thirty and thirty-five propositions laid out by the last three speakers, all of which are researchable propositions. To research doesn't mean that you put off action, but that you put research energy, fund, and legitimacy into a subject. And the subject in this case is conflict. I don't think the subject is disarmament; disarmament follows circumstances in which we are in conflict. But I am willing to argue that with you. The need for massive movement of research capacity in this direction is the clearest thing in the world. J. David Singer, in a letter to the *Washington Post* some time ago, estimated that there were at least sixty to seventy thousand of our highest-grade intellectuals making better weapons of killing and refining them and that there are perhaps one hundred first-class minds in the United States concerned with conflict and its management and maybe three hundred in the world. And there are a lot of second-class minds like my own on it, maybe another three or four hundred.

But that is a disportionate thrust in our research direction. If we are really concerned about security, which is a concern if we think of security in terms of the welfare and well-being of peoples, and perhaps even the integrity of their states, the fastest way toward security is, of course, peace research or research on the conditions of peace—how we can quarrel and dispute and have conflicts without killing each other.

As a matter of fact, the peace-through-strength thing needs revising, and we can call it a strength-through-peace movement, which I think is cost effective. One more thing I have to say about the research function in the conflict field, beside its being quite new and very underrepresented, is that as soon as you start doing it, the objects of research start behaving differently. We have gone to riots and we have gone to civil disputes, scheduled ones particularly, with people with notebooks, and the people in dispute start acting differently. We had fifty old ladies in tennis shoes in Miami Beach with notebooks, and every time someone started raising Cain, these people took their notebooks out and started writing in them, and it cooled the scene. They were doing research. They were getting good results, and this was an unintended consequence of a research program down there. Your twenty-three propositions that you laid out as possible things are all researchable. So, I just wanted to finish my list and also make a plea that, in terms of our research and development functions, there is a mass of R&D that has to do with the welfare of a country and world that is fairly easily steerable as soon as you can show that security increases. Perhaps the highest cost benefit from R&D funds that you can put in is a way not to fight.

Phillipe de Seynes: I think that the title of this colloquium is right because it indicates that disarmament is a problem of society at least as much as of government. Although, I would say that the word "societal" is rather dubious. If it is a problem of society, I think it is legitimate—as I understand some speakers have done—to place it in a wider context. And certainly, it must be placed in the context of North-South relationships much more than has been done today. It is just possible that the mechanisms to preserve peace and a certain degree of equilibrium in armaments are better assured than the mechanisms to organize the North-South relationship and to promote the development of the South. I am suggesting this as a hypothesis. Most of the things which have been said here have been normative and incremental. And I don't know that I have anything more or better to offer in this connection. But I think that if one tries to extrapolate from experiences in certain less acute conflict situations than those we face in the global problem, then I have also my doubts here. We have to deal in this problem with the most powerful forces, and I think we have to recognize them. And if we can do no more, at least we should try to expand our cognitive powers and understand them better. I do agree that this is also incremental.

But if we look at the social mechanisms that are at work, we must first look at one powerful social mechanism, which is the market. It exists and it plays its role in most of our societies, which live under mixed economies. We have neglected the market, as one tends to nowadays, because one has really such a shaky theoretical basis on economics that one plunges into voluntarist policies without looking too carefully at the context in which they have to take place. So I think that we have to look at the market much more accurately than we have done up to now. The market for armaments is a very queer market and a very special one. It is directly linked with other important markets, particularly to that of energy, but also of capital goods and, more indirectly, with manufacturers of food and other raw materials.

In the studies which the UN system is undertaking now on long-term objectives, I am afraid that this may not receive sufficient attention. It didn't in the previous UN model, although the so-called Leontief model did recognize differences between oil importing and oil producing countries. But it didn't push investigation of the relationship between this factor and the armaments factor. This is something which I think has to be taken into consideration when you are building scenarios, which will have to be scenarios of rapid industrialization, therefore of rapid growth, with satisfaction of basic needs and better distribution of income around the world. If one doesn't take into account the armaments problem there, one misses an important point. Naturally, when you talk about economics, again we face our shaky theoretical basis because we have not been able to incorporate into economic analysis the social elements which are now so determinant in so many fields. I suppose we should also make an effort to understand them.

I like the word that Saul Mendlovitz used of a "social movement." I don't know much about sociology, but I do believe that it is a key word in the sociological analysis of countries. We cannot nowadays speak of class and class conflicts as we did even fifty years ago. The identification of social movements—wherever they are, the way they operate, the way they are motivated—would be important. I do believe that there subsists and exists a workers' movement, in spite of its frequent complicity with the upper class and the establishment. I am also old enough to remember the origin of socialism in Europe, and one of my great distresses is the vacuum of thinking which exists at present in the socialist parties of Europe. And as one who voted for them in the recent election in France, I was distraught because I couldn't believe in what they were saying and proposing. We have to keep social movements in mind and try to look at their conflicts, their utopias, what they mean, and so on and so forth.

Now, finally, coming to action and institutions. This also comes from a social reflection, because we must not look just at groups. When we have to deal with the military-industry establishment, it is perhaps interesting to look into individual psychology. The other day I was in Vienna for a conference. Having one hour before my plane, I went to the apartment where Sigmund Freud had lived from 1891 to 1938. I was quite intrigued by the whole thing and the memorabilia. I was intrigued also by Freud as a subject of analysis rather than as the agent of analysis. There is a letter written by him when he was mobilized in 1914, and it is a decent but pretty straightforward nationalist statement. On the eve of the Second World War, there was the well-known correspondence between Freud and Einstein, which indicated some evolution in the whole series of fantasies which occupy the minds of people. Now, fantasies in the military establishment are very important to identify. I am neither a psychologist nor sociologist, but I suppose they play a great role.

I think Professor Osgood said, "I am going to say something horrifying." I would like to say something horrifying now too. The best agents for such causes as disarmament and peace are probably the smugglers of the Daniel Ellsberg and Jack Anderson type. I think very few things have happened as convincing as the episode of the *Pentagon Papers* during the Vietnam war.

Disclosure, exposure in a society that is organized like the United States, is a powerful weapon, a very powerful weapon, and it will naturally raise the level of insecurity for the politicians. But that is all to the good.

Fernando Ley: I would like to make a few remarks in the light of previous speeches, particularly referring to overkill capacity, elimination of nuclear weapons, unilateral disarmament, and so forth. I think that all of these are desirable objectives. However, and in this I disagree with a number of previous speakers, we cannot lose sight of the need for security. And at this point in time, I would like to introduce a few propositions, clearly meant to stimulate further our discussion.

It has been true since the beginning of history that peace among states depends on the maintenance of the balance of power. Precisely, security depends on international peace, international peace depends on international stability, and international stability depends on balance of power. So if peace depends on the maintenance of the balance of power, which is largely a military power, then surely it is safer for governments to pursue the objective of the balance of power deliberately. This is the case in the SALT negotiations, for instance. The purpose of arms control is then the attainment of a stable balance of power at a lower rather than a higher level. However, I must state that détente cannot be achieved only by the reduction of arms; hence, the need for a global strategy for peace, which I have already mentioned this morning. Many speakers have expressed here the need for nuclear disarmament. Of course, nuclear weapons have indeed a high priority. But at the same time, we cannot afford to lose sight of the serious threat caused by an ever-spiraling accumulation of conventional weapons. In fact, the peace and security of all states can rest only on a balanced reduction of both nuclear and conventional weapons. So if we agree that this is the only practical physical approach, let us see how we can accelerate the extremely slow efforts toward disarmament.

David Singer: As I've listened to the last day and a half of discussions I've been trying to find the appropriate synthesis for the very diverse views we've heard. I think many of you, in your own comments, have pointed out that there is a great deal of underlying consensus. Let me make a small effort in this direction. The first item on my agenda is that of the relevance of research. As Dr. Wedge will tell you, I probably take second place to nobody in this room in believing that we do not have nearly enough knowledge to know what kinds of policies on the part of which kinds of actors will produce what consequences. We are very much in the dark, and this is why I think it is terribly important, as has already been suggested, to expose at every opportunity the relative incompetence of national governments. I think the world ought to know that these men and women know not what they do. Therefore, any time we have a chance to challenge, question, and ridicule the dubious assertions and the contingent forecasts that we get from political *elites*, we should do so. That, of course, requires that we be vigorous, alert, articulate, and I suppose I'd even have to say, courageous. Those characters who work on that transmission belt, the people of the media, with all the technology that we talk about, are still human beings making decisions about what kinds of information gets to what kind of people and when. The technology will do us no good as long as the agents of the contemporary political elites have a stranglehold on those channels. Now we can break through that in several ways. As Elise Boulding suggested, we can try to bypass them, and the technology to some extent permits this. But another thing we have to do is give them a quick and dirty education, and one way to give them an education is to call them to task. One of the things I've spent a lot of time doing the last thirty years is dashing off quick, somewhat sarcastic letters to reporters and TV commentators when they've been wrong. If I did it every time they were wrong, I would have no time for teaching or research. For example, just yesterday *The New York Times* had a story describing some of the contemplated changes in American military strategy. It was a very incompetent piece of work. The reporter who wrote it has no sense of what has gone on in the last thirty, sixty, or three hundred years. He was essentially writing what he was told. He was writing off "boiler plate," a combination of what he was told and what he was handed in some mimeo-graphed releases. But if I'm the only man in the United States of America who writes to these characters, then this means we're not doing our job. I strongly suspect I am the only one, because when I meet these people, when I talk to them on the telephone, they say, "Well you're the only person who ever said that I was incorrect on this."

This leads in turn to the question of the role of values. These people, the media people, the opinion makers, the elites, and unhappily all too often the counter-elites, are accepting certain implicit values when they compare and analyze the values of different policies. For example, one of the basic sets of value underlying the real American military doctrine today—and similarly, Soviet doctrine, it goes without saying, and by extension virtually that of all the governments of NATO and Warsaw—is that nuclear weapons no longer exist only to deter the other side's use of nuclear weapons. Of course, we have moved back and forth, as I suggested yesterday, somewhere between first- and second-strike doctrines. No major power since the early fifties has had a pure second-strike doctrine. Every one of them has always had a mix that includes a large component of a "fight-the-war" doctrine and a "win-the-war" doctrine. These days, of course, both the Soviets and the Americans are showing all the signs of moving back up toward a doctrine of "fight the war and win the war."

One of our jobs, because we are more knowledgeable and more competent, is to raise these issues. But now what's happening? There's a big debate going on, not only in the United States, but in the USSR, as to the relative merits of alternative strategic doctrines, what kinds of weapon systems you buy, how many of each weapon class you get, where you deploy them, and what you say about them. We, as usual, will sit quietly by and let this set of decisions be made by a small handful of relatively competent, highly interested, very parochial characters. Then we will be presented yet again with another *fait accompli*, and we'll be that much closer to nuclear war. We're not talking about disarmament tomorrow morning. We're talking about slowing down, capping, and then beginning a long, gradual incremental downturn in the militarization of the world. But I will bet you that nobody in this room will utter a public statement that will be heard by more than fifteen people on the extent to which American military strategy, and by extension that of America's allies, makes arms reduction and arms elimination that much more difficult and that much less likely. What I'm saying is that it may be beautiful for us to talk about the "New International Economic Order," and it would be beautiful to talk about how nice the world would be as values change, as the allocation of resources change, and as people become better in touch with themselves and one another. Fantastic. But as "peaceniks" we've got a couple of concerns, and the number one concern is to find some scenario that links the world as it is and the world that we would like to see.

We have different notions of what the utopias would look like, and that's fine. But we should all have a fairly similar and accurate picture of what the world looks like now, and we should be challenging the decisions on a day-to-day basis in terms of our notions of utopia and in terms of our notions of how we get there. Now if Saul Mendlovitz wants to use military force, to shed blood, in order to hasten the day when blacks govern themselves in South Africa, that's nice. I wouldn't do it. I would be opposed to it because I know from history that blacks can oppress blacks just as well as whites can oppress blacks, and I'm not about to use force punitively to achieve a desirable social outcome. I think that most of us have to become a lot more pacifist, but we ought to become a lot more vigorous intellectually and much more knowledgeable empirically.

My closing comment, then, is that we ought to have a pretty clear notion of what our various utopias look like and we ought to have disagreements on that. We ought to be debating them all the time. But we ought to recognize where the world is now, what is the distribution of power, what is the distribution of beliefs, what are the preferred outcomes that people are pursuing, what strategies and tactics are they using, and who has hands on what kinds of levers of power. We should begin addressing these people today. And it seems to me that the very first step for those of us who belong to the nations in the Western alliance had better make it public that every single component in western military doctrine is moving us further and further away from peace. Therefore we've got to know something about military strategy. We have to know the difference between weapons that are essentially first-strike and those that are essentially second-strike. We've got to be ready to call the bluff of the hot air artists who stand up and say, "Listen, Mister, if you knew what I knew you wouldn't ask that naive question." The word "naive" has been thrown at me at least fifteen times in the last day and a half, and probably fifteen thousand times in my career. Why is it naive to suggest that maybe rational individuals can come together collectively and not necessarily arrive at irrational, dysfunctional, maladaptive strategies. I'd say one way we handle this is to begin to address the immediate situations without ever losing sight of the future.

Ervin Laszlo: One of the things that has come out of this afternoon's discussion is that we ought to be doing more than one thing at the same time. We cannot afford to be talking only about security or only about disarmament, only about social movements or only about theories, only about the practical steps—what's feasible. We ought to be doing all of these things practically, at the same time. As Garrett Harding says, in reality you cannot do just one thing. When you do only one thing, it always has untold consequences and its feedback keeps coming back to you. Except for a few forums like this one, we are still organized to do only one thing at a time. If meetings deal with disarmament, they think it is an issue that can be handled by itself. Actually, I think if you want to deal with disarmament and security, you ought to handle it in the broadest possible context, because it's not a military issue and it's not even primarily a political issue. Sure, the solutions have to be political, and finally the solutions have to be military, but these solutions will have to come somehow from a transformation in society. That means education, that means getting on to the people, that means the psychological factors, and that means we will have to emphasize the economic factors.

Now, two things just occurred to me at this point. One, we ought to bring these complex sets of issues to the public attention simply as much as possible. I was very late to lunch for the following reason: I was asked only two days ago to appear on a talk show at one o'clock this afternoon. I couldn't resist it because it was an opportunity to talk about some of these things. They said, "You will be done in five minutes." Well, we were on the air for forty minutes. Somehow they found it interesting to talk about the dangers and talk about the problems, and so on, and how can you change values. We ought to do more of these things. I kept pressing the need for the media to get more involved in these things, and those people said, "Alright, maybe we ought to have programs like this every week." And this sort of thing, perhaps, could be done.

Second, in these settings here, like at the UN, perhaps we ought to pay more attention to the interconnections of these issues. When we discuss disarmament, we oughtn't to only discuss economic issues in terms of funds liberated from disarmament for development. That's a surface manifestation that will never occur unless there is some amount of economic equity developing that will permit nations to feel secure in the absence of the tremendous levels of arms. So whenever we talk of disarmament, we ought to talk about the New International Economic Order; whenever we talk about the New International Economic Order, we ought to be talking about the armament situation. We talk about industrial development and so forth. We will have a UNIDO Conference coming up. We will have UNCTAD V coming up. We will have a science and technology conference coming up. Then we'll have the Special Session on the New International Economic Order coming up. All of these things ought to be brought together so that, finally, the element of peace and the conditions that could lead to peace—namely, the removal of perceived injustice—could gradually be rectified. As long as people have as many grievances as they now have all over the world, there's very little chance that any positive movement can occur. So I'll just end with a kind of a plea to bring in all the complexities of the issues in as complete terms as possible.

Morton Deutsch: Professor Laszlo and Professor Singer said much of what I would have wanted to say. At this point I just want to add one note which I don't think has been sufficiently emphasized in our discussions. I feel that we have not sufficiently focused on the resistances to movement toward the kinds of objectives that we all have been describing. I think we have very well characterized some of the things that have to be accomplished, but we have not talked about how you develop the political interest that favors movement in that direction. There is a political interest that clearly favors the continuation of an armaments race, the continuation of massive military expenditures. We, if we are going to be serious about our commitments to moving in the direction we all espouse, have to ask, "How do we develop a countervailing political interest that fosters movements in the direction that we want to attain?" We, I think, are clear on our ultimate objectives. But to move from where we are toward our ultimate objectives, we have to seriously enter the political process and political analysis in terms of our understanding of how interests are formed. I'm a psychologist, not a political scientist, but I think these political issues have not been adequately addressed in this kind of meeting. I would hope that in future discussions they will become an important element, because so long as we stay at the level of ultimate objectives, we will not be practical.

Saul Mendlovitz: I have spent the last twenty years, like David Singer, learning the numbers, mapping, MIRVing, MARVing. I sit in the Council on Foreign Relations, and I'm invited to the inner group on disarmament, so if you want me to spew the numbers at you, I will spew the numbers at you. My experience has been very chastening. I don't think any amount of information I will give them will be new. Even when I said I'm ACDA and have the information, because we just have a different view of the risks and the national security interests of the United States, my desire to go to a social movement is not thrown out frivolously. I do not believe that politics as usual will handle the resistances in this society.

When I think of the movements that I know best because they're in Western civilization, Christianity and communism, they required a total commitment and life-style. Planetary citizenship is of such a nature, and so I meant it in that serious a vein because I honestly do not believe in sitting around and coming to the UN, which I can stand maybe three times a year, and listening to people who have to act on behalf of the nation-states as representatives. The way they act out these national interests in these forums is enough to let you know that the system is so encapsulating and crushing that you can't do anything.

So, to get back to your point, I don't see a way to handle either the resistances or the rational things by the usual letters to the editor, by the usual going to our congresspeople. I just spent a couple of weeks down in Washington, D.C. talking to all the liberals about the probability of getting those people to take seriously the notion of some disarmament, radical system change, and things of that sort. "Where is the constituency?" they ask. "Where are the people out there? Who's going to vote for what you want?— After all, there's been only a 3 percent real increase in military spending." So I think the situation is much worse than David thinks it is. I think the resistances are much worse.

When I go with Daniel Ellsberg to get arrested in nuclear protests, I do that only because the thing is too crazy. It seems to me that we're at that point. These resistances in all societies are so strong, they are so systemic that I don't see how you do it with the usual kinds of things that we talk about. You have to say it enough out loud until you finally force yourself into being a fool and acting foolishly, and then that turns into being courageous. That's what I mean by a social movement: that somehow or other you really force yourself into the frame of mind, attitudes, and feelings where you really begin to do things that are Gandhian, that are John Garrison, whatever it is that will force the structures to really begin to move. And honestly, David, I don't think that all your rationality is going to change by 2 percent anything those guys are going to do. And they're all guys; there are few women.

O. W. Markley: I just want to ask a fairly simple question that might lead to something operational. Maybe it's already been proposed and may be under way. The International Institute for Applied Systems Analysis (IIASA) was presumably set up as the kind of forum through which people could come together and act in that way which, again and again in this discussion people have said, in terms of the things they've seen happen in the past, always works best: experts coming together in a way that they can behave as experts, not as representatives of their own sovereign nation-state at a place where they can essentially act, not only as experts, but as planetary citizens. Has this vehicle ever been chosen as a place to look at these questions in terms of the larger sense of strategy? What do we do with the nuclear question? If so, what has happened?

David Singer: They don't permit that item on their agenda.

O. W. Markley: I wondered if it was that political.

David Singer: I was instructed very explicitly on that.

Elise Boulding: You were instructed. Well, I would say that there are people who participate in that who would very much like to put it on the agenda. I'll give you the names and addresses of three of the women who are part of that who would be very glad to do it.

O. W. Markley: Might that be a fairly straightforward action step that is graspable?

Paul Lin: I've been very impressed with a lot of the very careful studies that have been made, and have learned a great deal. I would like to place myself firmly, however, on the side of those who believe that disarmament should not be an isolated study, completely insulated, so to speak, from the realities, the political realities. I seem to sense a tendency to do that because it seems easier for us to neutralize the question of disarmament—to make it into something in which we can enlist the widest public opinion, so to speak, including the public opinion of those who are perpetrating the armaments race—and I would like to suggest that there is a danger in the question of armaments and disarmament so that we don't have to ask the question when we use words like "security." Whose security, for what and by whom? And when it comes to questions like armament, whose armament, for what, by whom? If we don't ask these questions, then it's a very academic, abstract discussion and the world will roll on toward its destruction.

It seems to me that the dynamics of armament, as the dynamics of destruction, and of disarmament have to be attached to these realities. We've discussed a lot of norms, and the only norm seems to be whether one arms or disarms. But it seems to me that armament is an *instrument* of policy; not policy itself; not in a basic essential sense. So we're talking really about phenomena rather than essence if we're talking only about armaments. The fact is that the use of armaments in a predatory fashion is really the most serious question that we face, because when we're talking about issues such as the end of the world and so forth, what are we talking about? A fight between Tanzania and Zambia? Or are we talking about something quite different qualitatively?

It seems to me that when there is a growing tide of opinion that war is coming on a world scale and we are talking about disarmament, there is something wrong with the logic there: on the one hand, it seems logical that the world should disarm; on the other hand, it's illogical, because if war really is coming, what government can you persuade to disarm? So to me the much more basic issue is to find what those dynamics are that are moving us toward war, and to try to correct them. First of all, we can of course improve the international system in such a way as to slow down, if not eliminate, those dynamics. These are involved in questions which relate to how a superpower, especially, or any expansionist nation, gets expansionist, and in the present context of the world as it stands to see where the greatest danger lies. Otherwise, it's academic discussion for those who make policy. Of course, in the long run, as far as the institutional and value systems are concerned, it seems to me that this lies in the long-run struggles that we are talking about—where we first of all, on the international scene, try to eliminate, to withdraw those elements which make possible the struggle for power, the extension of influence, and so forth; for example, the nonaligned movement, such as the zones of peace; to help and support these movements as part of the question of disarmament. In a very much longer run, it seems to me the necessity is to encourage through the dissemination of public information and so forth those internal movements which eliminate or tend to eliminate tendencies toward national chauvinism and all those internal social movements which eliminate or tend to eliminate the disparities between people, particularly the disparities of power within societies. If we look in that long-range and historical perspective, it seems that it would be much closer to the reality than if we see disarmament as an isolated phenomenon unrelated to these realities.

William Epstein: I had no idea that the questions asked by Professor Lin were things that people here would be worried about. I was going on the assumption that nobody here believed that disarmament could be divorced from political reality or could be dealt with in isolation. I don't think that there's a single person here who would support that thesis. And if people have not brought that out, I think that they're just taking it for granted that everybody here accepts it as fundamental. I agree that basically what most people talk about in the United Nations when they talk about disarmament is to hold back the superpowers and their mad arms race. But not them alone. The superpowers have developed a theory of deterrence. Now they talk about détente. And I suppose most people do accept that over the past thirty years deterrence has played a role in preventing the outbreak of a big nuclear war and that, with détente developing the way it is, there is less danger of an outbreak of a war now than there was before. The problem is not that the superpowers are going to have a war by design or by intention. I think the problem is that deterrence is not going to work. It never worked in history for long, and it's not going to work indefinitely now. The danger is that there will be a war by inadvertence, not by intention. A big global war is the result of accident, miscalculation, human or mechanical breakdown, inadequate command, control and communication, nuclear terrorism, or escalation of a local war. Little local conventional wars, if they acquire competing superpower interest, can become something major, unwittingly and unwillingly.

The problem is also the proliferation of nuclear weapons. It's not that the smaller powers are less responsible. It's that they don't have all those sophisticated, second-strike, invulnerable retaliatory capacities: they don't have the sophisticated electronic locks, permissive-action links, and physical security systems, and the dangers of an accidental war will be vastly multiplied as these weapons proliferate. That is the danger.

When it comes to the arms race, you say we ought to know the factors of it. Well, you mentioned several of them. A lot of these people here talked about them for a day and a half, but mentioned them just casually. The arms race has got a dynamic and a momentum of its own. It's no longer the action-reaction process, although that enters the picture. It's no longer just the perceptions of fear of what the other side intends. That is an element of it, but the thing goes on of its own accord now. They're on a treadmill. They don't know how to stop it. It's linked with the internal economy and it's linked with politics. Eisenhower said it: the military-industrial complex and, what most people forget, the scientific-technological elite. He could just as well have added the bureaucratic complex and the labor one.

I don't think it's fair to say that we're talking about disarmament divorced from reality, political reality. The point is so few people are talking about disarmament or arms control that those of us who are interested have to zero in and emphasize it; otherwise, nobody will talk about it at all. That, I think, is the problem, and that's why I think that this whole colloquium was called, so that we will talk about disarmament and international security in a societal context. I hope I'm not being unfair in saying that there are many things which we did not talk about or did not raise because we felt that they were being taken for granted. I, for one, think that maybe the whole world needs psychoanalysis or something. Or all of the military and industrial people and most of the scientists do. Now, scientists are decent people, except that science may be neutral while scientists aren't. To use another figure, it's been estimated, depending on how you define it, that 25 to 50 percent of all the scientific and engineering brains and people of the world are devoting their energies to weapons-related work. About 40 percent of all R&D goes into military work. That's one of the reasons that we have inflation and imbalances—economic, financial, and fiscal—and currency imbalances and unemployment as a direct result, too. I think most of these things are known. The problem is, how are you going to get people to deal with them? I thought that's what most of us are trying to talk about. And you know it's not easy. Those of us who have been knocking around in this field for a generation, I assure you, know the problems. I suspect that we know more about the difficulties and the problems than those who have been on the fringes of the disarmament work. We have run into them every day for thirty years. The problem is, how are we going to move on from where we are?

Jerome Frank: I am suffering from a bad case of intellectual indigestion at this point. We've heard so many generalities and so many exhortations about things most of us really knew already that I don't quite know where to break into this. I think the problem is what Mr. Epstein just said, what do we do about this? I don't think we're going to get anywhere by exhorting each other to do things we can't do. I can't go out and change the social structure of the world, improve great power relationships, and so forth. Perhaps some of you diplomats can. It seems to me that each of us has to select one place that he can get into. For me the cutting edge has come up several times. I have to make one generalization. I think we may have missed one of the big problems of instability in the world—which is the energy problem. The standard of living of every society depends on its energy level. Energy levels are declining with reference to the population; therefore, the standard of living in societies is going to go down: therefore, internal tensions are going to increase. We haven't dealt with that, and that's going to increase the whole international insecurity. We haven't dealt with that one at all.

I'd like to say that the one place I can see to get into this, because I belong to a group that is interested in this, is the matter of the economics of the arms race. As has been brought out, unions are beginning to get interested in this. The massive military-industrial complex is a little shaky now because it's becoming clear that so many of our scarce resources are being diverted to them—something like 70 percent of our oil is really going to military; something wild like this. That's too much, but it's an awful lot. That may be a place to get into it.

May I at this point ask one specific question that's been haunting me ever since Mr. Spek spoke. I don't know if I understood him correctly. It's simply this: I thought you said that no nuclear war can begin unless the aggressor controls outer space. Am I misquoting you?

Yaap Spek: No.

Jerome Frank: Well, doesn't it leave out of account the irrationality of people?

Yaap Spek: I tend to believe that it is true from what I said before in my speech that command and control are of utmost importance to doing anything.

Jerome Frank: But the world leaders say that unless we control outer space, we're not going to start a nuclear war? Is that what you're saying? I just wanted to make clear that I understood you.

O. W. Markley: Is that because of the ABM potential from outer space?

Yaap Spek: Yes. The control function, everything, has moved to space. That's what it's really about.

Jerome Frank: Can we knock down interballistic missiles from space now?

Yaap Spek: I don't know. I wish I knew more than I do, and I'm trying to find out. But it's very clear to me that the whole battle has moved to the electro-magnetic battle-field which takes place in outer space.

Jerome Frank: Well, thank you. This was just a clarification.

Chadwick Alger: I don't think you ought to say that arms races have a dynamic of their own. I think that's a mistake. What you're saying is that the dynamic is not really explainable with respect to external relations. It is not a dynamic of its own. It's a dynamic that's mixed in with jobs for labor, for scientists, and so forth. It is not a dynamic of its own, and I think we aren't disagreeing about the fact, but I think that the semantics are important there. The fact that it isn't a dynamic of its own gives us some handles.

Bryant Wedge: The National Peace Academy campaign is going to go on for two years. It's going to push the idea that war is not inevitable, that making peace is possible. It's going to be a very public campaign, and we're going to go after both the American and the international audiences very hard and fast. I think that's a step along the road, whichever road we're taking in this direction. So I'd like to invite a lot of collaboration. I was going to quote Eisenhower correctly because he said, "Only an informed and knowledgeable citizenry can *compel* the proper meshing of our giant industrial and military machinery of defense with our peaceful methods and goals so that security and liberty may prosper together." That's a very splendid statement, and he put the action where it has to be. He said, "Only an informed and knowledgeable citizenry" can compel this. All the action to make things change, would have to come through the mobilization of citizenries, of political action.

People compel governments; and I think any progress in this field has to depend on the understanding that the governments who are holders of the monopolies of power must be compelled by their people to change. I happen to know that Eisenhower and MacMillan had a little exchange, and MacMillan said, "Yes, Ike, it will only happen when the people take our weapons away from us." And that's where it will happen, I believe. And it can be done.

Geoffrey Pearson: I do not think it is helpful, whatever our goals are, to speak in terms of "us" and "them"—the government is all bad, and the public or whatever is good. Some officials are competent and some are incompetent, some are moral and some are immoral, and certainly in the question of arms control, there are all kinds of competing constituencies in government. Obviously, the military have great influence, but there are other areas of government where you have officials, and indeed bureaucracies, which are looking for the same kinds of outcomes as you are, or most of you. Perhaps what it is important to do is to find within government—this is one way that the citizenry is going to influence the politics of any country but on the more discreet level—those groups and those constituencies that can be helpful. But if you blanket government in ways that I've heard today, with the kinds of suspicions and so on, you will turn officials, who can of course be helpful, against the whole thing. You're starting from a way down, anyway, because public opinion plus government is mostly on the side of defense, security and so forth. So unless you can call for help to groups and officials who can be helpful, you're going to make it all that much more difficult.

Piero Vinci: I would like to say what I feel is the conclusion of this very large and very interesting debate. First of all, we are all aware that the time is short, that we are in a mad world in which we seem to be on a collision course, and we are putting out these questions. How can we avoid this collision course? How can we stop the dynamics? I use the word "dynamics" of the arms race in the plural because, as a matter of fact, it involves so many factors and interests. At the same time, it's the adversities we are facing—how to overcome all these hurdles and obstacles in the way that are so great. I think we are also aware of the difficulty of demilitarizing the world and trying to create a new world where we can all live in peace, cooperate, and solve the real issues, the real global challenges of our world. But I think the input we have here is so good and so great that we have at least the knowledge and the awareness of the intricacies and the complexities of arms control and disarmament, since it's connected with everything—every part and everything in life. It's connected with security. It's connected with the economy. It's connected with social life. It's connected with learning. Perhaps this is the message which could come out from this colloquium; to shed the light to all people, in our own countries and elsewhere, of these connections and these complexities, and try to mobilize public opinion—to try, as Professor Mendlovitz has spoken about, to mobilize the social forces, if he had this in mind.

There's so much to do, and so little time. But, at the same time, if this is the message which comes out from here, I think it would be useful. At least we would give one contribution, with this real conscience that all is linked and that we have to face and try to solve all of the problems at the same time. I think it's really a gigantic sort of task, but this doesn't mean we should not try altogether. And I hope that Donald Keys with his collaborators and friends could produce some of the recommendations which could be used in several forums, and perhaps we, personally and associated with others, will try to do our best to mobilize public opinion and try to fight against these big obstacles which our constituencies' interests represent. But if we can raise the consciousness of the people and show that this is the danger we are running, then there is hope. If all of us do what we can in mobilizing public opinion, perhaps we can make some progress, if not succeed at once.

Index

161

PARTICIPANTS

Chadwick F. Alger	Professor, Director, Project on Trans-National Intellectual Cooperation in the Policy Sciences, Mershon Center, Ohio State University at Columbus
Elise Boulding	Professor, Department of Sociology, Dartmouth College, Hanover, New Hampshire
George Brown	Professor of Education, Program Leader, Graduate Program in Confluent Education, University of California at Santa Barbara
Alessandro Corradini	Former Deputy to Assistant Secretary-General, Center for Disarmament, United Nations
Morton Deutsch	Professor of Psychology and Education, Teachers College, Columbia University
William Epstein	Special Fellow, UNITAR, Member, Canadian Delegation to the UN General Assembly
Jerome Frank	Professor Emeritus of Psychiatry, Johns Hopkins School of Medicine, Baltimore, Maryland
H. E. Fereydoun Hoveyda	Former Permanent Representative of Iran to the United Nations
Donald Keys	President, Planetary Citizens
Ervin Laszlo	Professor, Special Fellow and Project Director, UNITAR
Fernando Lay	First Secretary, Mission of Italy to the United Nations
Paul Lin	Professor, Centre for East Asian Studies, McGill University, Montreal, Quebec, Canada
O. W. Markley	Associate Professor, Studies of the Future Program, University of Houston, Clear Lake City, Texas
Saul Mendlovitz	Director, World Order Models Project, Institute for World Order, New York

Robert Muller	Secretary, Economic and Social Council, United Nations
Davidson Nicol	Executive Director, UNITAR; Under-Secretary-General, United Nations
Charles Osgood	Professor, College of Communications, Institute of Communications Research, University of Illinois, Urbana
Geoffrey Pearson	Director-General of Bureau of UN Affairs, Ottawa
H. E. Carlos Romulo	Secretary of State for Foreign Affairs, The Philippines
Phillipe de Seynes	Director, Project on the Future, UNITAR
Yaap K. Spek	Research Engineer, Center for Advanced Computation, University of Illinois at Urbana
J. David Singer	Research Political Scientist, Mental Health Research Institute, University of Michigan, Ann Arbor
Inga Thorsson	Undersecretary of State for Disarmament, Ministry of Foreign Affairs, Sweden
H. E. Piero Vinci	Permanent Representative of Italy to the United Nations
Bryant Wedge	President, Institute for Study of National Behavior, Alexandria, Virginia